NORTH AMERICAN YF-93
BY WILLIAM SIMONE

INTRODUCTION: North American's oft-forgotten YF-93A was an advanced version of the F-86 Sabre, first being designated as the F-86C, being the natural follow-on to the F-86A day fighter, that promised superior capabilities. It featured an advanced inlet system, a J48 centrifugal compressor afterburning engine and three times the fuel, promising to give it extremely long range. In its original configuration it failed to deliver, suffering from a poor performing inlet and high drag. These problems were fixed and test flown, but it is unclear if the USAF evaluation boards ever considered the data. Because of the original configuration issues, the YF-93A has been classified as a failure. This book is an attempt to present the newly discovered flight test data and clear the air.

It is very difficult to establish a timeline for the F-93 program as many documents have been lost or destroyed over the years and the few that remain have conflicting information. No formal written reports were released on the YF-93A's Air Force Evaluation and the NACA files, minus two technical reports, consist of two photos and a footnote. Even the North American Aviation archive records held by Boeing are thin.

PENETRATION FIGHTER PROGRAM CONCEPT: The concept of a "penetration fighter" evolved towards the end of WW II, when the USAAF anticipated the need for a new class of jet fighter aircraft for the long-range escort of its strategic bombers. The term was used to describe a theoretical long-range fighter aircraft designed to penetrate enemy air defenses and attack defensive interceptors. The concept is similar to the escort fighter, but differs primarily in that the aircraft would not operate in close concert with bombers.

The desire for a fighter that could penetrate enemy airspace along with the bombers led to an USAAF Invitation to Bid on 28 August 1945. Tentative Military Characteristics for the Penetration, All Weather and Interceptor type fighters were disseminated to the industry late in

August 1945 with request for proposals by the Air Material Command (AMC).

After technical evaluation contracts were awarded on 1 April 1946 by Headquarters USAAF, Washington DC, for the Penetration Fighter to McDonnell's XF-88 and Lockheed's XF-90 proposals. For complete Penetration Fighter Program details see Air Force Legends 222, Lockheed XF-90.

ENTER THE YF-93: North American Aviation (NAA) entered the competition in a very unconventional fashion. In December 1947, North American Aviation (NAA) submitted its design for consideration, well after Lockheed and McDonnell were on contract, giving it a disadvantage in the competition. In addition, although the AMC penetration fighter specifications

Above and below, early F-86C (YF-93) concept illustrations showing F-86A type wings and tail mated to a new fater fuselage with NACA intakes to incorporate the J48 engine. (NAA/Boeing via Mike Lombardi)

had established the need for two turbojet engines, NAA felt that a single, high-power engine would benefit their design. The Pratt & Whitney J48-P-1 engine chosen to power the aircraft was a license-produced, Rolls-Royce Tay engine, and utilized a single-stage centrifugal compressor and a single axial-flow turbine. Being a centrifugal compressor design, it was much wider than the General Electric J47 engine used in the F-86A. The J48's diameter was 50 inches vs the J47's 39 inches. The J48 required a plenum while the J47 required a direct duct to the engine face. This forced the NAA design-

ers to come up with an entirely new fuselage to be mated to the F-86A wing and tail unit. In addition, the fuel load was to be 3 times that of the F-86A. The increased weight of the design then led to a redesigned undercarriage, and increased armament also ruled out a nose

Before the YF-93 entered the Penetration Fighter Program, the McDonnell XF-88 and Lockheed XF-90 were under construction. Above, the two McDonnell XF-88 prototypes at St. Louis. (Ginter collection) Below, overhead view of the large XF-90 in flight. (Erik Simonsen)

mounted, engine intake at an early stage. With this design configuration finalized, NAA proposed its model NA-157 as the P-86C to the USAF on 20 September 1947 and also put forward the design to fulfil the all-weather interceptor requirement.

On 1 December 1947, NAA proposed that 190 F-86Bs, on order under contract W33-038-ac-16013, should be cancelled in favor of continued F-86A production and two P-86Cs under the same contract. On 20 February 1948, the USAF issued an order for two prototypes (serial numbers 48-317 and 48-318) as contract W33-038-ac-21672. The Air Force ordered the F-86C into production solely as a penetration fighter. On 22 March 1948, a revision to the contract finalized the side-mounted engine intakes, and a further change on 29 March reflected the deletion of external fuel tanks.

NAA then submitted a proposal on 9 April 1948 for the two F-86C prototypes at a fixed price of $6,811,449, plus 118 additional F-86C production aircraft. The Air Force agreed with this proposal and authorized North American to proceed on 29 May 1948, to include spares and production tooling.

At this time, it was decided that there was so little commonality between the F-86C and the production Sabre that the aircraft should be assigned a new designation. Thus, in late September 1948 the design was changed to F-93 with the two prototypes being designated YF-93As.

On 12 January 1949, a partial termination at the convenience of the Government reduced the quantity on order from 119 F-93As (F-86Cs), plus one static test article, to two YF-93A flight test articles. In the renegotiation of the contract, the two YF-93As were now at a price of $7,329,816 and a further $4,167,568 to cover spares, data and support equipment.

At this time the Air Force stated that no production order for further penetration fighters would be awarded until a competitive fly-off between the three contenders, XF-88, XF-90 and YF-93A, had taken place. This must have been a shock to NAA for they had managed to secure a production contract just to have it canceled in short order for the convenience of the Government.

2

According the Duncan Curtiss, "Despite this, the USAF placed a further order on 5 May 1949 for one F-93A as an all-weather fighter. Given the contract number W533-038-AC-21672 and the NAA designation NA-166, this anomaly came to naught shortly afterwards when the contract was cancelled, no doubt as a result of the plethora of other designs by then coming "into production.

The first YF-93A was completed at Inglewood in late 1949 and trucked to Edwards AFB in December for ground testing and taxi tests in preparation for its maiden flight.

At this time, both the XF-88 and XF-90 had been flying for months, the XF-88 having made its first flight on 20 October 1948 and the XF-90 on 3 June 1949. The first flight of the YF-93A would not occur until 24 January 1950.

AREA RULE AND THE YF-93A: It has been written in many publications that the YF-93A did not have an area rule fuselage, but the high level structural drawing and overhead photos of the aircraft clearly shows that it did. The reason given is that "area rule" had not yet been discovered. That is very much in error.

At high-subsonic flight speeds, the local speed of the airflow can reach the speed of sound where the flow accelerates around the aircraft body and wings. The speed at which this development occurs varies from aircraft to aircraft and is known as the Critical Mach Number. The resulting shock waves formed at these zones of sonic flow cause a sudden increase in drag, called wave drag. To reduce the number and strength of these shock waves, an aerodynamic shape should change in cross sectional area as smoothly as possible from front to rear.

The area rule says that two airplanes with the same longitudinal cross-sectional area distribution have the same wave drag, independent of how the area is distributed laterally (i.e. in the fuselage or in the wing). Furthermore, to avoid the formation of strong shock waves the external shape of the aircraft has to be carefully arranged so that the cross-sectional area changes as smoothly as possible going from nose to tail. At the location of the wing, the fuselage is narrowed or "waist-

YF-93 FUSELAGE STRUCTURE

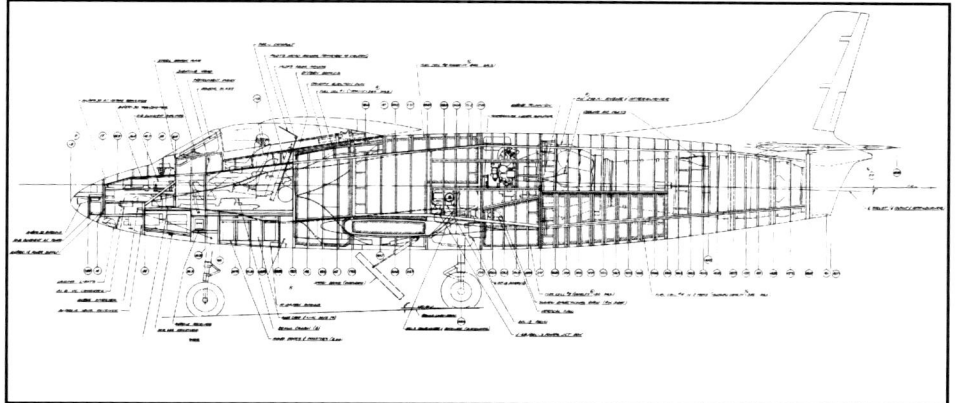

NORTH AMERICAN YF-93 CUTAWAY

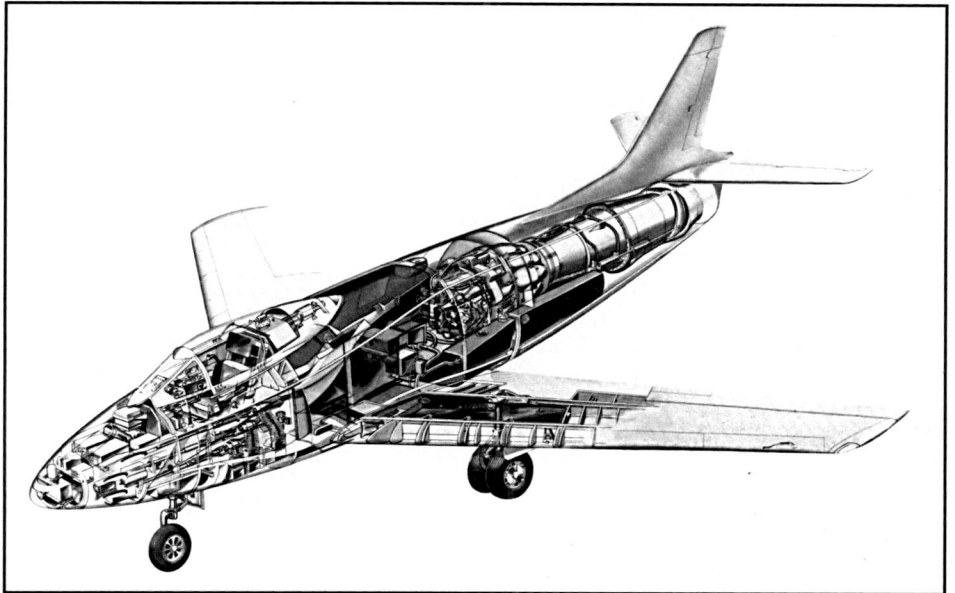

NORTH AMERICAN YF-93 EXPLOADED VIEW

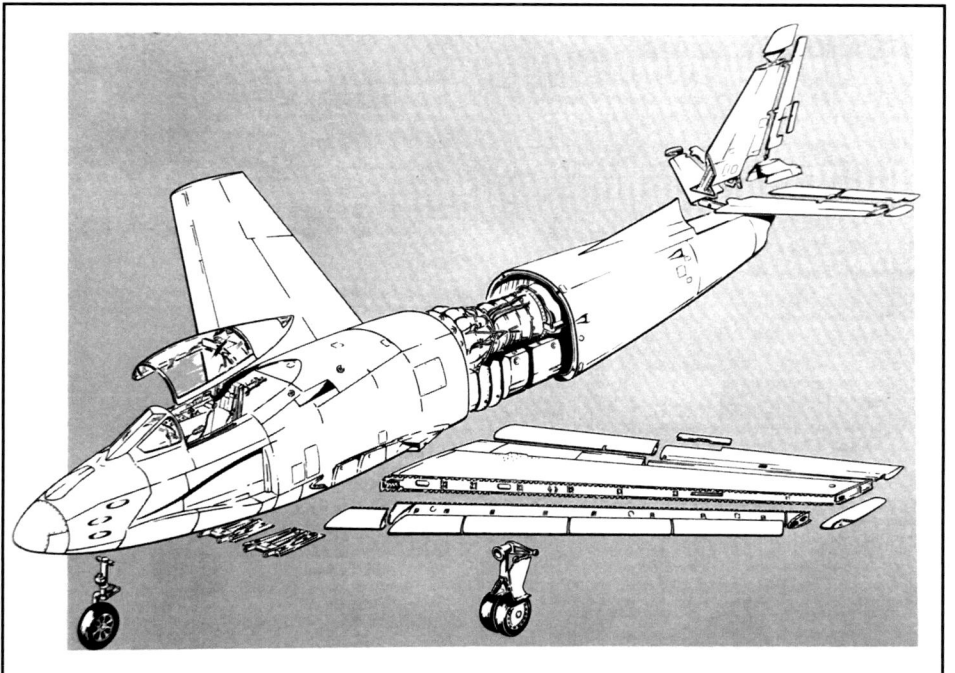

3

17 October 1947	North American initiated a design study of an afterburning version of the F-86.
1 December 1947	North American proposed that 190 P-86Bs, on order under contract W33-038-ac-16013, should be cancelled in favor of continued P-86A production and order two P-86Cs under the same contract.
17 December 1947	North American starts production engineering for two F-86C aircraft, pursuant to an advance Contract Change Notice substituting two F-86C's for the last two P-86B's then on order under contract W33-038 ac-21672.
20 February 1948	Contract Change Notice No. 32 to Contract W33-038-ac-16013 authorized production of two F-86C aircraft.
22 March 1948	The revision to the contract was finalized.
29 March 1948	A change made to reflect the deletion of external fuel tanks.
9 April 1948	NAA proposed two P-86C prototypes at a fixed price of $6,811,449, plus 118 additional P-86C production aircraft.
29 May 1948	An order for 120 F-86C aircraft, plus spare parts and tooling was received from the Air Force.
24 August 1948	A static test article was substituted for one of the 120 articles in a revision of the F-86C order.
September 1948	Mockup was inspected and approved by USAF during the week of 20 September.
30 September 48	Model designation was changed from F-86C to F-93A.
12 January 1949	A partial termination at the convenience of the Government reduced the quantity on order from 119 F-93A's, plus one static test article, to two YF-93A flight test articles.
25 February 1949	Fixed Price Contract W33-038-ac-21672, authorizing production of two YF-93A aircraft, spare parts, etc., was approved.
28 February 1949	Basic release of YF-93A engineering drawings was made to manufacturing.
December 1949	Delivery of the first article, 48-317, to Edwards AFB.
24 January 1950	First Flight of the first YF-93A 48-317.
28 March 1951	Program Termination.

ed".

The area rule was discovered by Otto Frenzl when comparing a swept wing with a w-wing with extreme high wave drag while working on a transonic wind tunnel at Junkers works in Germany between 1943 and 1945. He wrote a description on 17 December 1943, with the title "Anordnung von Verdrängungskörpern beim Hochgeschwindigkeitsflug" ("Arrangement of Displacement Bodies in High-Speed Flight"). This was used in a patent filed in 1944. The results of this research were presented to a wide circle in March 1944 by Theodor Zobel at the Deutsche Akademie der Luftfahrtforschung (German Academy of Aeronautics Research) in the lecture "Fundamentally New Ways to Increase Performance of "High Speed Aircraft.

Several other researchers came close to developing a similar theory, notably Dietrich Küchemann who designed a tapered fighter that was dubbed the "Küchemann Coke Bottle" when it was discovered by US forces in 1946. In this case Küchemann arrived at the theory by studying airflow, notably the interference, or local flow streamlines, at the junction between a fuselage and swept wing. The fuselage was contoured, or waisted, to match the flow. The shaping requirement of this "near field" approach would also result in Whitcomb's later "far field" approach to drag reduction using his sonic area rule. It is likely the benefits of this drag reducing method was discovered by NAA when they were able to review the highly classified captured German WWII documents and built on it.

In the United States, Richard T. Whitcomb, after whom the rule is named, independently discovered this rule in 1952, many years after the YF-93A was designed, flown and nearly retired, while working at NACA. His research was done using the new Eight-Foot High-Speed Tunnel, a wind tunnel with performance up to Mach 0.95 at NACA's Langley Research Center.

STRUCTURAL DESIGN: The North American YF-93A was a prototype single place, swept wing fighter, not a demonstrator. Little details on the YF-93A structure has been found, but it is known to have been based on the proven F-86A design and methods. Much of the structure was semimonocoque. Monocoque is a structural system in which loads are supported by an object's external skin, in a manner similar to an egg shell. The term semi-monocoque or semimonocoque refers to a stressed shell structure that is similar to a true monocoque, but which derives at least some of its strength from conventional reinforcement such as longitudinal stringers and ribs.

The wing, fuselage and empennage were of all-metal construction with the exception of composite type material used on the vertical stabilizer tip and radome. The fuselage was a semimoncoque structure in two sections with a break point at Fuselage Station 297 for removal and servicing the Pratt & Whitney J48 turbojet engine. Access doors in the fuselage made most areas accessible for repair and maintenance. The 35 degree sweptback wing was made up of a center section and two outer wing panels. The outer wing panels were mated to the center section by bolting bars. The wing was attached to the fuselage at four points. The wing center section and outer panels to Wing Station 126 contained fuel cells.

The empennage consisted of a 35 degree sweptback, trimmable horizontal stabilizer and elevator, a 35 degree sweptback fixed vertical stabilizer and a rudder. Conventional rib and skin type structure was used.

The landing gear was fully retractable tricycle type, with the main gear retracting into the wing and fuselage and the nose gear into the fuselage.

No Structural Design Criteria documentation has been found, but based on a Flight Restriction Notice dated 2 April 1951, the following limits were established for the aircraft:

1), Do not lower the landing gear or flaps above 230 KIAS.

2). Do not exceed Mach 0.95 or 580 KIAS below 25,000 feet. Above 25,000 feet there were no speed restrictions.

3). Landing at a gross weight in excess of 18,900 pounds should be made cautiously.

The maximum permissible G loads were as follows:

Gross Weight Lbs	Maximum Permissible G	
	Level Pullout	Rolling Pullout
28,750	4.6	3.5
	3.5*	3.4*
26,500	5.0	4.0
	4.0*	3.7*
21,850	5.0	4.9
		4.5*

*Above Mach 1

Detailed Description of the Fuselage Structure: The YF-93A fuselage structure was an all-new design based on proven F-86A methods and practices. It was made from 2024, 7075 aluminum and corrosion resistant steel being used in areas that saw high temperatures. The fuselage was of semimonocoque construction. Four main longerons carried the bending loads and the stressed skin carried the shear loads.

The fuselage was built in three major sections – forward, intermediary and aft. The forward and intermediary sections when permanently mated was then referred to as the forward fuselage. The forward fuselage and aft fuselage mated at fuselage station 297, referred to as a field break for engine removal, service and inspection. This allowed the entire aft fuselage to be removed.

The forward fuselage section contained the radar, radio and electronic equipment, armament and ammunition. Also contained in the forward section was the pressurized cockpit, inlets, nose gear wheel well and speed brakes. The speed brakes, unlike the F-86A, were on the lower fuselage, their approximate leading edge was hinged at the projected intersection of the wing leading edge on the fuselage centerline.

The wing was attached to the forward fuselage by four tension bolts at the intersection of the wing spars to the fuselage.

The aft fuselage contained the engine and afterburner shroud. It was designed to withstand the higher temperatures of engine operations. Four union-type threaded couplings at quarter-points around the fuselage held the two sections together. The shear loads were transmitted through the joint by shear pins in matching holes around the circumference of the two matching frames.

All hydraulic lines and fuel lines were connected through self-sealing bayonet-type pull-away connections.

The aspirator assembly was considered a nonstructural fairing and did not contribute support to the fuselage or empennage structure. Its primary function was to provide satisfactory airframe cooling throughout the aft fuselage section. The aspirator

was constructed of corrosion resistant steel.

THE YF-93A NACA FLUSH INLETS: NAA decision to use the NACA flush (submerged) inlets on the F-93 design was based on NACA wind tunnel testing and technical reports that showed good pressure recovery and low drag. The inlet of a jet aircraft functions to capture and decelerate air prior to entry into the compressor of the jet engine. While the inlet is often

optimized for cruising conditions, it must provide adequate mass flow during all other engine operating conditions including takeoff, landing, and maneuvering. The design of a high speed aircraft inlet system is a very complex and challenging engineering task.

A great deal of NACA's work was to support research on external and internal aerodynamics including inlet and duct systems. As part of this work, NACA

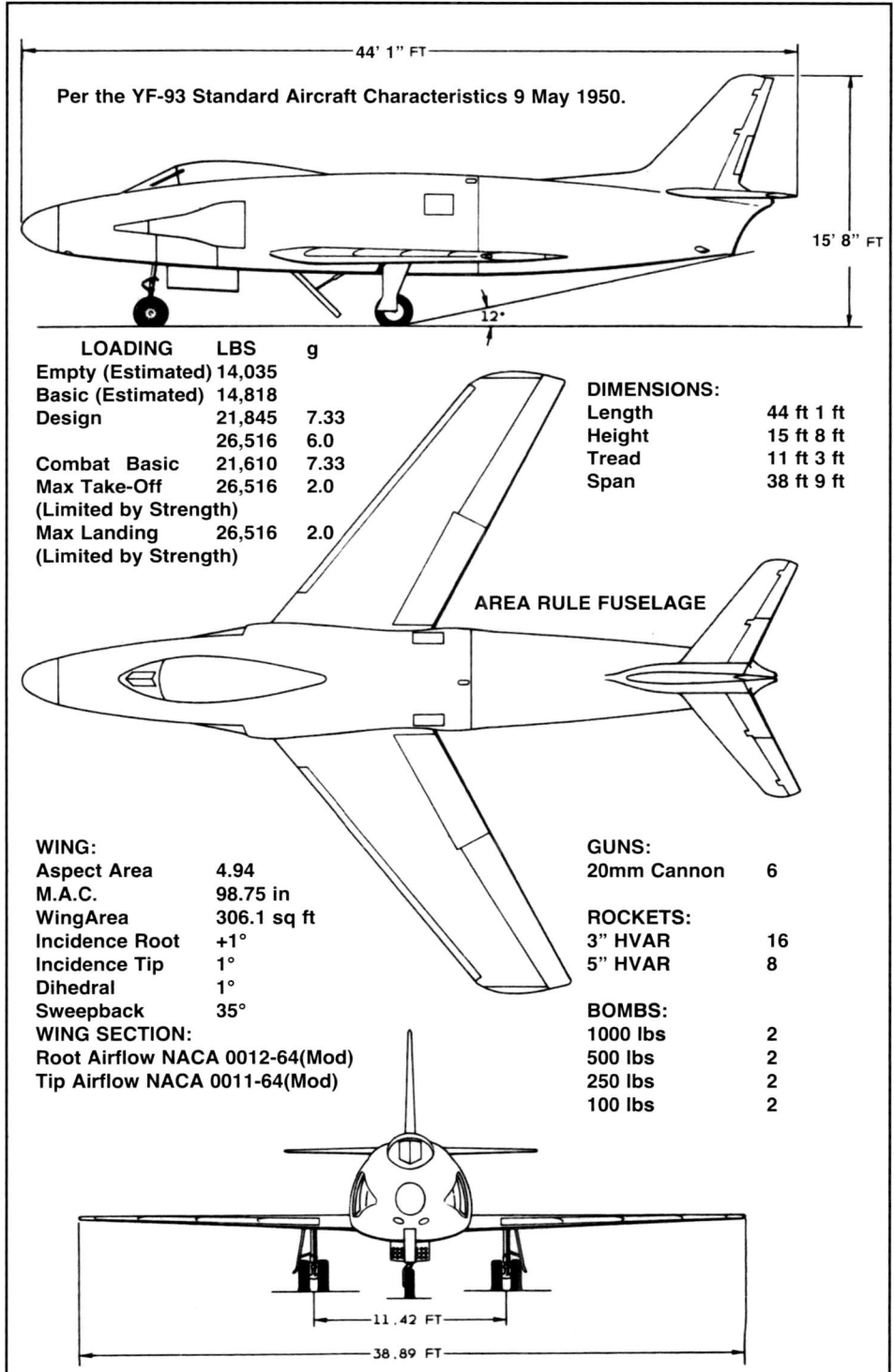

Per the YF-93 Standard Aircraft Characteristics 9 May 1950.

LOADING	LBS	g
Empty (Estimated)	14,035	
Basic (Estimated)	14,818	
Design	21,845	7.33
	26,516	6.0
Combat Basic	21,610	7.33
Max Take-Off	26,516	2.0
(Limited by Strength)		
Max Landing	26,516	2.0
(Limited by Strength)		

DIMENSIONS:

Length	44 ft 1 ft
Height	15 ft 8 ft
Tread	11 ft 3 ft
Span	38 ft 9 ft

AREA RULE FUSELAGE

WING:

Aspect Area	4.94
M.A.C.	98.75 in
WingArea	306.1 sq ft
Incidence Root	+1°
Incidence Tip	1°
Dihedral	1°
Sweepback	35°

WING SECTION:
Root Airflow NACA 0012-64(Mod)
Tip Airflow NACA 0011-64(Mod)

GUNS:

20mm Cannon	6

ROCKETS:

3" HVAR	16
5" HVAR	8

BOMBS:

1000 lbs	2
500 lbs	2
250 lbs	2
100 lbs	2

5

Walk around of the number one YF-93 on Rogers Dry Lake in December 1949 with original flush (NACA) inlets and original aspirator. Armament was not installed on the first YF-93, S/N 48-317. (Ginter collection)

Ames conducted follow-up testing for tests conducted at NACA Langley in 1941. The NACA Ames report, "An Experimental Investigation of NACA Submerged Duct Entrances" was published in October 1945.

It appears this very important sentence would be missed by various aircraft man-

Above, the unmodified flush inlet on the first YF-93 at North American's Los Angeles Airport (LAX) facility. Below, two views of the modified flush inlet after the tuft survey of Flight 13 on ship one. Wind tunnel tests determined the optimum inlet duct configuration. Results of these tests indicated that straight ramp fairings with rounded edges leading into the duct entrance had less drag than the original ramp fairing. (Ginter collection)

ufacturers.

PREVIOUS AIRCRAFT DESIGNS THAT USED FLUSH INLETS: The YF-93A was not the first jet aircraft to fly with the NACA flush (submerged) inlets.

It is a little known fact that Lockheed also attempted to use the NACA flush inlets in 1946. XP-80B 44-85200 was modified to the XP-80R high-speed configuration. The canopy was smaller, the wings were shortened and their leading edges were re-contoured. In its initial configuration, the XP-80R retained the J33-A-17 engine, and incorporated new NACA flush intakes.

Quoted below are sections of the technical report: "The National Advisory Committee for Aeronautics, working closely with the Army and Navy, has been conducting extensive research on the problems of jet-motors air-induction systems at its various laboratories. Results of this research concerned with fuselage-nose inlets and external scoops have been published…"

"As a part of this research program, the Ames Aeronautics Laboratory has undertaken the investigation of air inlets submerged below the surface of the body into which the entrance is placed. This type of air inlets is not new, have been tested first during the duct-entry research of Internal-Flow Systems for Aircraft, NACA Report 713, 1941. Submerged and semi submerged inlets have also received considerable attention of various aircraft manufacturers. It is the purpose of this investigation reported herein to provide more complete information on entrances of this type so to define their relative merits compared with other types of inlets."

"…the results of the general investigation were applied to a specific airplane design and test of a 0.25-scale model in the Ames 7x10 foot wind tunnel number 1. The airplane used for this purpose is a high speed fighter airplane powered with a Halford jet motor. From the results of the basic research, twin submerged entrances were designed to supply air to the Halford unit at an inlet velocity of 0.70

[Mach] at an airspeed of 475 miles per hour at 15,000 feet altitude. The internal ducting was of constant area back to the twin entrance of the jet motor. Pressure losses in the ducting as determined from bench tests were found to be 10 percent of the dynamic pressure of the air flowing in the duct."

Conclusions from the report: "In conclusion, it should be stated that submerged entrances have a definite advantage over inlet types for certain inlet and air-flow requirements."

"The results of a preliminary investigation of submerged duct entrances are presented. It is shown that an entrance of this type possesses desirable critical speed and pressure recovery in a region of low incremental velocity and thin boundary layer. The data obtained indicate that submerged entrances are most suitable for use with internal flow systems which diffuse the air only a small amount: for example, those used with jet motors which have axial flow compressors. Where complete diffusion of the air is required, fuselage nose or wing leading edge inlets may prove to be superior."

"Drag. – No drag measurements were made in the general investigation in the Ames 1 by 1.5 foot wind [tunnel] channel. It is impossible to distinguish between the external and internal drag of a submerged inlet in the same manner as for an inlet in the leading edge of a wing or streamline body. Nearly all of the air which suffers a loss in momentum due to the presence of the submerged inlet flows into the entrance of the duct where that loss in momentum appears as a pressure loss. For the basic submerged duct, it might be said that external drag is a negative quantity since there probably is an improvement of the flow behind the inlet because of the removal of the boundary layer."

"It is expected, however, that the use of deflectors will result in some small external drag, but in view of the large increase in pressure recovery resulting from their use, it is believed they will result in a large net gain."

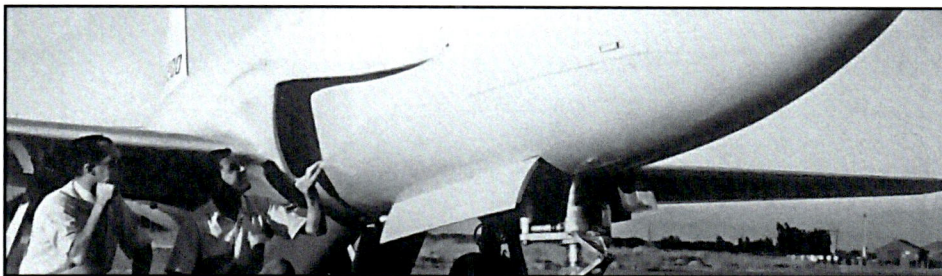

"Submerged inlets do not appear to have desirable pressure recovery [As fluid (air is this case) as velocity slows down, local pressure increases, i.e. pressure recovery] characteristics for use to supply air to oil coolers, radiators, or carburetors of conventional reciprocating engines. The required diffusion of the air and the range of inlet velocity ratio too great to give desirable characteristics at all flight conditions. It should be noted from a plenum chamber, fuselage nose inlets may prove to be superior to submerged inlets insofar as pressure losses are concerned." It appears this very important sentence would be missed by various aircraft manufactures."

The initial performance of the XP-80R was disappointing. The intakes were returned to the standard shape and the J33-A-17 was replaced by a J33-A-35 engine. The failure of the NACA flush inlets to perform was not shared within the aviation community.

Republic Aircraft also tried them when they modified the third XP-84A prototype with a more powerful J35-GE-15 engine and a pointed fairing over its nose intake, replacing it with NACA intakes on either side of the nose. It failed to meet the requirements set forth and was dropped

Above, XP-80R with NACA flush inlets at Lockheed Van Nuys, CA, in September 1946. (Simone collection) Bottom, third XP-84A with a more powerful J35-GE-15 engine and NACA flush inlets. (Kaston collection)

for further consideration.

The attempts to use the NACA inlets and their failures apparently were kept secret as even NACA Ames got this wrong. In "SP-4314 Atmosphere of Freedom: SIXTY YEARS at the NASA AMES Research Center," they state that the YF-93 was the first aircraft to fly with the NACA flush inlet.

On the North American YF-93A prototypes, the novel air intakes did not work either. North American tried modifying the ducts in various ways, including rounding the entrance somewhat. Eventually, they replaced the submerged inlet with a conventional ram inlet.

Today, we see flush inlets everywhere, and they are widely used in precisely the applications as engine induction and cooling air inlets, oil radiator inlets, fuel tank vents, and cabin ventilators, for which the original researchers deemed them unsuitable, but not for high speed jet inlets for which NACA said they were excellent for.

WING STRUCTURE

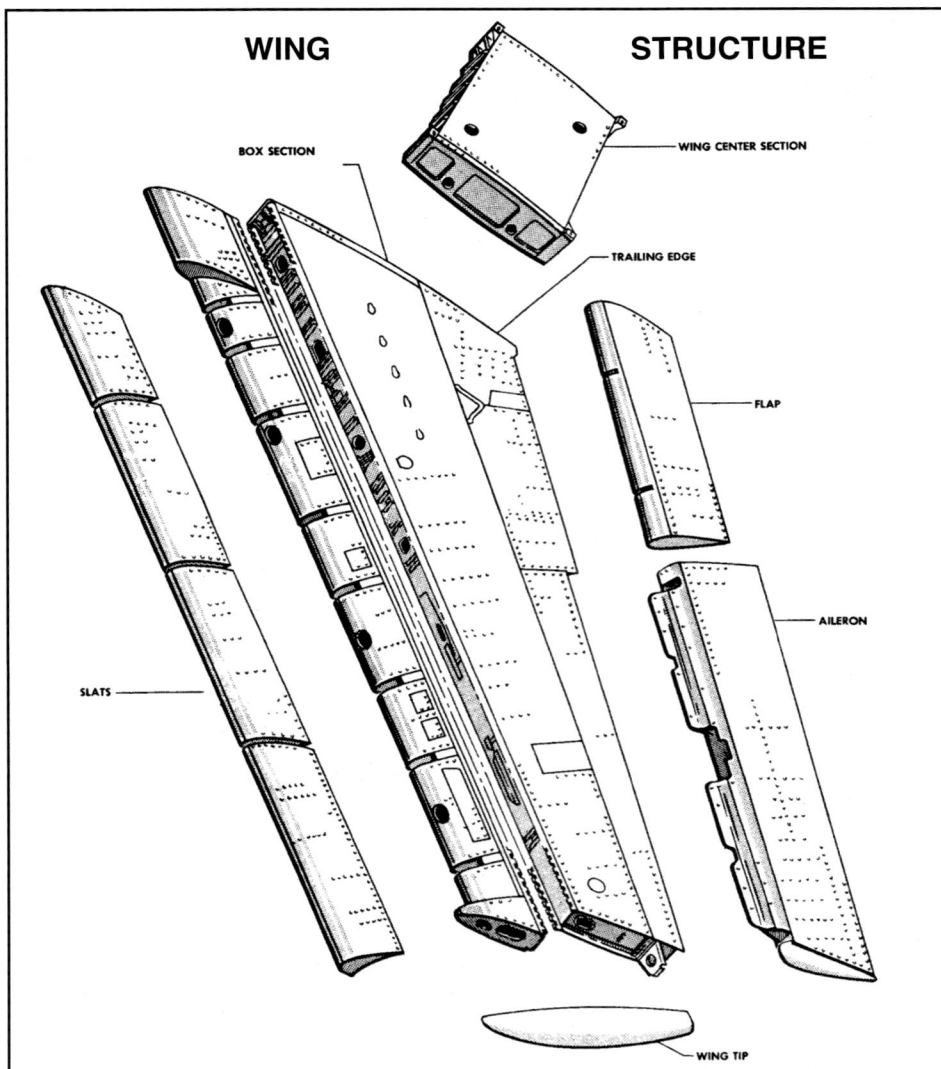

Labels: BOX SECTION, WING CENTER SECTION, TRAILING EDGE, FLAP, AILERON, SLATS, WING TIP

DETAILED DESCRIPTION OF WING STRUCTURE: It is believed, based on very limited information, that the YF-93A wing was based on the F-86A wing structure beefed up where necessary to take the higher loads caused by the additional weight. The wing was a full cantilever, sweptback wing of all metal semimonocoque design. The wing was a two spar structure consisting of two outer panels and a center section. The center section and outer panel contained rubber fuel bladder tanks.

In the fuel cell bays, a double skin was used with stringers separating the inner and outer skin. On the outer panels, a single skin structure was used outboard of Wing Station 126. Wing skins were tapered spanwise. All external skin riveting was dimpled or machine countersunk flush types resulting in a smooth low drag surface.

The landing gear trunnion was attached

directly to the rear spar, and a side brace. The trunnion fitting transmitted the landing gear loads to the wing.

The leading edge was a removable assembly attached to the front spar. A broached extrusion hinge jointed the leading edge to the hinge section attached to the front spar.

There were four leading edge slat sections on each wing. Each slat section was attached to slat tracks at two places. The slat tracks were bolted to the slats and run through rollers attached to the leading edge structure. The slat sections were flexibly linked together to move in unison without binding.

The slat structure consisted of a main spar, chordwise ribs and a trailing edge strip. They were covered by an aluminum alloy skin. The slat tracks were made from 4137 alloy steel.

The wing outer panel box section was formed by a front spar, rear spar, skin stringer cover panels and intermediate ribs. The wing box section carred all bending and shear loads. The center box section was formed by a front spar, rear spar and double skin upper and lower cover panels. The center box section attached to the fuselage by four bolts through the corner attach fittings.

The wing trailing edge assembly was secondary structure, fairing the wing outer panel box section to the ailerons and flaps. The trailing edge attached to the rear spar and was not removable as a unit.

The wing flaps were an all metal stressed skin construction, consisting of forward and aft spars, two longitudinal stringers top and bottom and chordwise ribs. It is believed that the skin was 7075-T6 aluminum alloy alclad sheet and the stringer made from 2024-T4 aluminum rolled stock. All ribs were press formed from 2024-T4 aluminum alclad sheet. The trailing edge was a magnesium alloy extrusion.

The ailerons were all metal, statically and dynamically balanced surfaces, attached to the wing by three antifriction type bearings. Static balance is the tendency of the control surface to remain stationary when supported from its own CG. Dynamically balanced control surfaces use air pressure to help move the controls by having a portion of the control surface in front of its own hinge to catch the passing air. This takes the load off the pilot's control mechanism. That way, the wind itself helps push the control surface into the position that the pilot has selected, making the controls feel lighter.

An aerodynamic seal was provided at the leading edge by means of a fabric strip attached from the leading edge (paddle portion) of the aileron to the wing rear spar. Ribs, spars and stringers were mainly made of 7075-T6 aluminum with skins made of 2024-T4 aluminum alclad sheet. The trailing edge was made of a magnesium alloy extrusion.

DETAILED DESCRIPTION OF HORIZONTAL STABILIZER AND ELEVATORS STRUCTURE: The all metal horizontal stabilizer design was made up of a center section and two outer panels. The outer panels were swept back at an angle of 35 degrees at the 25% chord. The outer panel consisted of two longitudinal spars, a trailing edge strip and transverse ribs. The outer panel nose skin, leading edge beam and ribs were fabricated from 2024-T4 alclad sheet. The main beam web, aft skin and the doublers were 7075-T6 alclad sheet. The main beam spar caps were machined from a 7075-T6 extrusion. The center section was made from a 7075-T6 extrusion.

The elevators were an all metal stressed skin construction, consisting of forward and aft spars, two longitudinal stringers top and bottom and chordwise ribs. It is believed that the skin was 7075-T6 aluminum alloy alclad sheet and the stringers were made from 2024-T4 aluminum rolled stock. All ribs were press formed from 2024-T4 aluminum alclad sheet. The trailing edge was a magnesium alloy extrusion.

DETAILED DESCRIPTION OF VERTICAL TAIL AND RUDDER STRUCTURE: The vertical tail surfaces consisted of a fixed stabilizer and a movable rudder with a trim tab. The surface was swept back at an angle of 35 degrees at the 25% chord.

The vertical stabilizer was semimonocoque design. It was all metal with the exception of the tip, which was plastic. It had three longitude spars, the aft of which was cut away in two places for the rudder counter-balance weights. The skin, leading edge spar, trailing edge spar, ribs and intercostals were 2024-T4 alclad. The main spar web was 7075-T6 alclad sheet. The main spar caps, intermediate rudder hinge fitting and outboard rudder hinge fitting were machined from 7075-T6 extrusions. The lower rudder hinge attachment fitting was machined from 2024-T42 extrusions.

The rudder was all metal structure except for the tip which was laminated glass fabric. It was attached to the stabilizer on three antifriction bearings. The rudder consisted of a box section formed by the beam, the side skin and trailing edge extrusion. The skin and ribs were fabricated from 2024-T4 alclad sheet. The beam and channel doublers were fabricated from 7075-T6 alclad sheet. The hinge fit-

tings and counterbalance weights were 356-T6 aluminum alloy sand castings. The rudder horn was machined from 4130 steel plate. The trailing edge was made from a 2024-T42 extrusion.

Static and dynamic balance of the rudder was obtained by means of weights attached to the outboard and intermediate hinge fittings, forward of the hinge line. The all metal trim tab had a single spar along its leading edge which also acted as a hinge to attach the tab to the rudder.

AIRCRAFT SYSTEMS: The YF-93A was a prototype of a production aircraft, not a demo aircraft like its competition and the design of its systems reflected this.

THE PRATT & WHITNEY J48: The YF-93A was powered by a J48-P-1 engine which produced an uninstalled thrust of 6,000 pounds dry, 8,000 pounds with afterburner. It was a continuous flow jet engine which had a single stage centrifugal flow compressor driven by a single stage turbine and was one of the first engines with an afterburner.

The Pratt & Whitney J48 (company designation JT7 Turbo-Wasp) was developed by Pratt & Whitney as a license-built version of the Rolls-Royce Tay. The J48 was a thirty percent enlargement of the preceding Nene/J42, and was produced both with and without afterburning. It was advanced for its day with a double-sided centrifugal compressor and nine tubular combustion chambers.

YF-93 TAIL STRUCTURE

J48-P-1 ENGINE AFTERBURNER INSTALLATION: On the YF-93A, thrust augmentation was provided by an afterburning type tail pipe. The afterburner unit incorporated a two position exhaust nozzle and a full regulating system. As the pilot's throttle lever was moved forward to the 100% throttle position, the afterburner fuel pumps were energized and fuel was fed to the afterburner fuel nozzles. Momentarily moving the throttle lever outboard at the 100% throttle position energized an electrical circuit which operated a fuel injector in one of the combustion chambers. Injection of high pressure fuel produced a torch-like flame which extended through the turbine wheel momentarily, and ignited the fuel in the afterburner

Below, mock-up of the J48-P-1 single-stage centrifugal flow compressor engine driven by a single-stage turbine and afterburner. (NAA/Boeing via Mike Lombardi)

Above, the J48-P-1 engine produced an uninstalled thrust of 6,000 lbs dry and 8,000 lbs with afterburner. (NAA/Boeing via Mike Lombardi) Below, access to the plenum chamber and engine accessories was through two large doors in the wheel well or through a large door in each fuselage side. Bottom, the aft fuselage could be removed for engine and tailpipe maintenance or for an engine change.

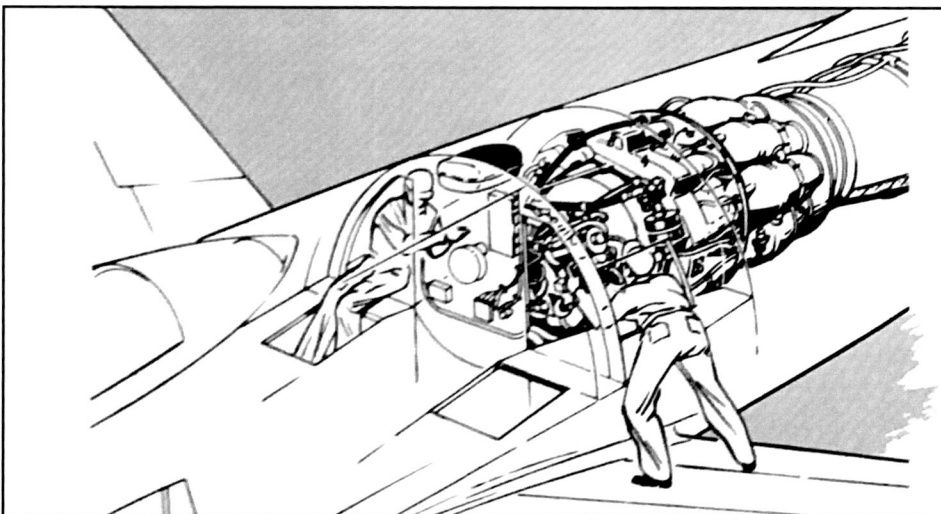

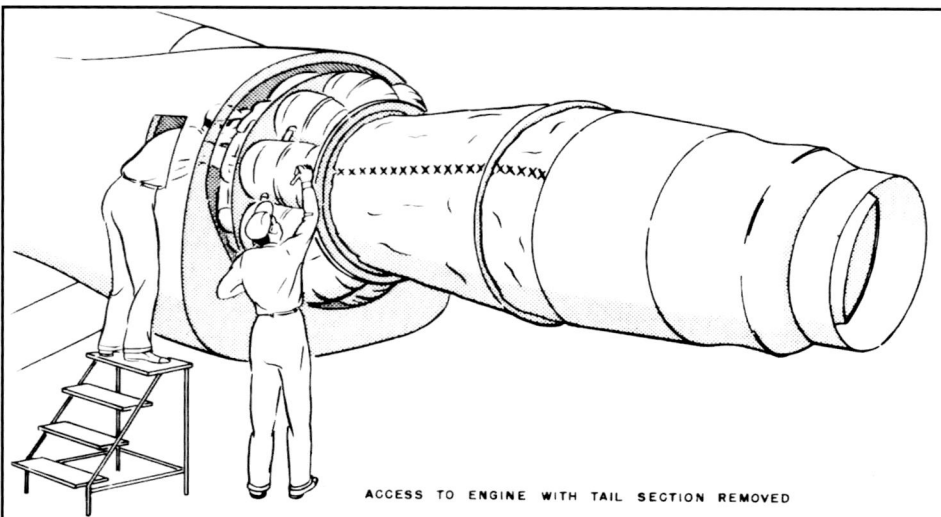

ACCESS TO ENGINE WITH TAIL SECTION REMOVED

unit. Combustion was then continuous until the fuel supply was cut off by moving the throttle lever aft.

The afterburner fuel flow was regulated to maintain a tailpipe temperature of 720°C. Although afterburner fuel flow was normally controlled by an automatic regulator, a manual controller was installed in the number 1 airplane for early flight tests so that the pilot could trim the fuel flow to maintain the proper tailpipe temperature.

Compressor discharge pressure, tailpipe static pressure, afterburner fuel pressure and engine driven fuel pump pressure was sensed by the device which controlled the exhaust nozzle actuator. The nozzle was maintained in the closed position for normal operation but opened for afterburner operation when the ignition of the afterburner raised the tailpipe pressure to a value high enough to actuate the exhaust nozzle actuator controller. This controller regulated the supply of compressor bleed air to the two pneumatic nozzle-actuating cylinders, located one on each side of the tailpipe. The pneumatic cylinders opened or closed the exhaust nozzle through a direct mechanical linkage.

With an aluminum airframe structure, the high temperature of an afterburner engine was a new challenge on how to keep structural temperature below the design limits of the materials involved. To do this NAA provided a cooling air system in addition to radiation shields.

The shields were in the form of a stainless steel shroud around the tail pipe extending from the afterburner mount flange to the aft end of the fuselage and insulation blankets around the tailpipe from the afterburner mount flange to the turbine wheel housing flange.

Cooling air was pumped through the aft fuselage by a two-stage ejector formed by the shroud and the fuselage tail fairing, which entered through four NACA flush type inlet ducts. Two of the inlets were located on either side of the fuselage at the firewall, and another pair was located at the forward end of the shroud.

POWER CONTROL SYSTEM: An engine-driven booster pump delivered fuel from the fuel tanks to three engine-driven fuel pumps. Two fuel pumps were necessary for satisfactory engine operation. The third operated continuously with the other two pumps and served as a stand-by in case either of them should fail. Fuel flow from all three fuel pumps was automatically controlled by a main fuel regulator in accordance with power control setting, engine speed, altitude, and airspeed. A wide-range rpm governor in the regulator maintained selected rpm and provided overspeed protection. If the main regulator should fail, an emergency fuel regulator was provided to take over engine fuel control. However, no automatic altitude compensation or speed control was provided by the emergency regulator, and extreme care had to be exercised in throttle movement to avoid overspeeding or exceeding temperature limits. A fuel stopcock, operated by the throttle, shut off the fuel supply to the engine when the throttle was retarded to the fully closed position. Afterburner operation was straightforward. When afterburner operation was selected, an electric fuel shutoff valve opened and an air-turbine-driven afterburner fuel pump delivered fuel from the fuel tanks directly to the afterburner. When afterburner operation was discontinued, the shutoff valve closed and the pump was shut off.

The throttle incorporated a stop on the quadrant at the "IDLE" position to prevent shutting off the fuel supply inadvertently when retarding the throttle. Outboard movement of the control (which was spring-loaded inboard) allowed the stop to be bypassed when the engine was being started or stopped. Initial outboard movement of the control from the "CLOSED" position closed a microswitch completing fuel booster and transfer pump circuits. The afterburner could not be put into operation when the switch was "OPEN", but once started, would continue operating when the switch was moved to "OPEN." The afterburner could not start if both generators failed, or if tail-pipe temperatures were excessive. If the afterburner was operating when either of these conditions occurred, it was automatically shut off.

FUEL SYSTEM: Seven self-sealing rubber bladder fuel tanks were installed in the airplane. Four were in the fuselage, a forward tank, a center tank, a main tank, and an aft tank and three were in the wing, a center wing tank and two outer wing tanks. All fuel was carried internally, there were no provisions for external drop tanks.

The total available fuel capacity was 1,581 gallons. The recommended fuel was 100/130 aviation gasoline.

AFTERBURNER OPEN

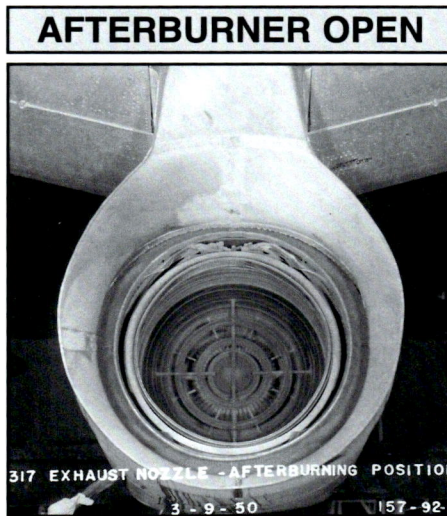

317 EXHAUST NOZZLE - AFTERBURNING POSITION   3 - 9 - 50   157-92-

AFTERBURNER CLOSED

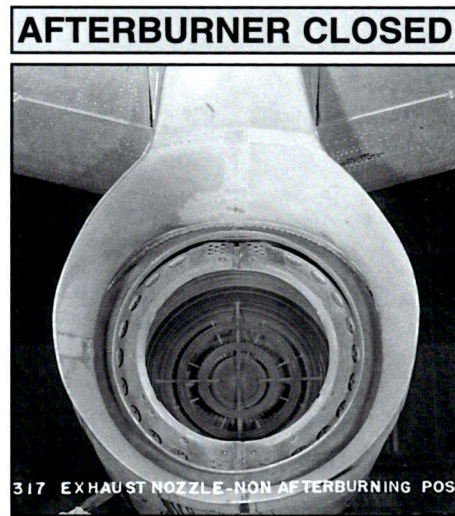

317 EXHAUST NOZZLE-NON AFTERBURNING POS

Normally, all fuel flowed into the main tank and was then pumped through a main tank manifold to the engine supply line. Forward, center wing, main, and aft tank fuel flowed under pump pressure, fuel from the center tank and outer wing tanks flowed by gravity feed. Because of the large spread of fuel in the airplane, fuel flow from the forward tank and the aft tank was automatically proportioned to maintain a correct airplane CG position.

A fuel gage, indicating total internal fuel in pounds, and a fuel flowmeter, giving rate of fuel flow to the engine in pounds per hour, were located on the instrument panel.

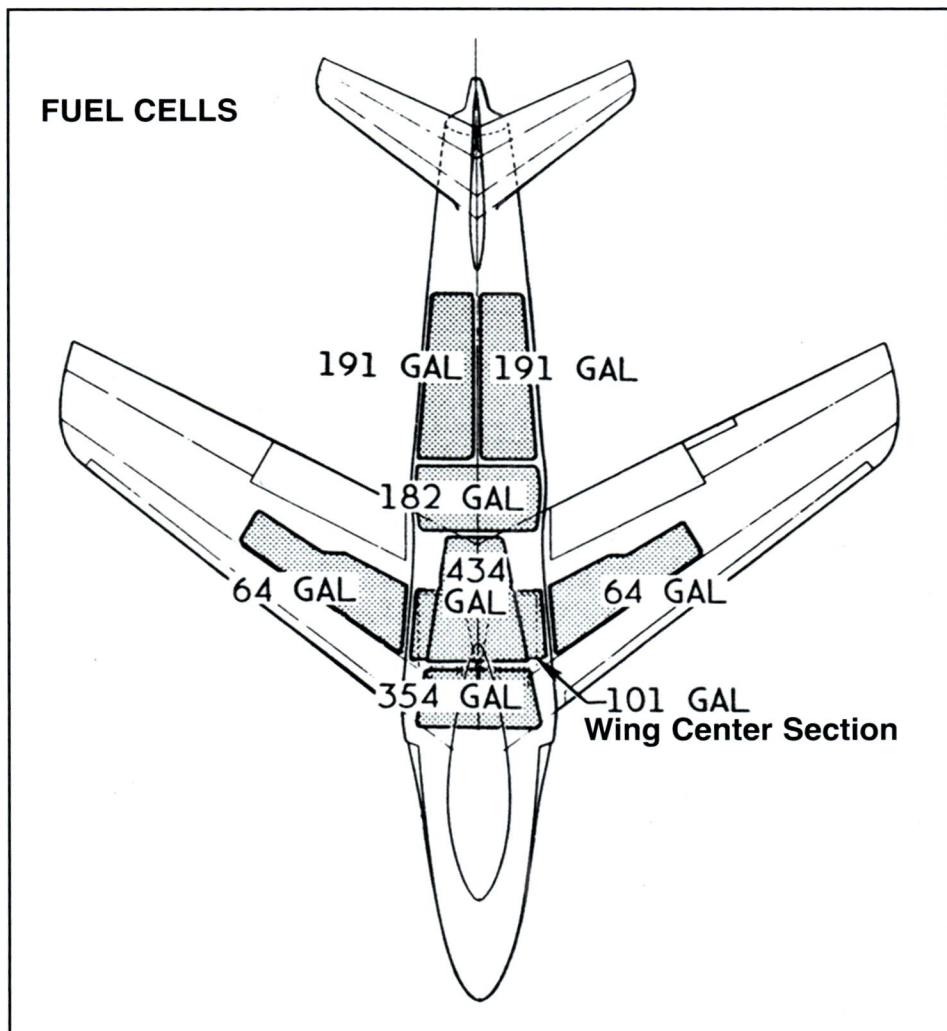

FUEL CELLS

191 GAL | 191 GAL

182 GAL

434 GAL

64 GAL | 64 GAL

354 GAL | 101 GAL
Wing Center Section

ELECTRICAL SYSTEMS: Electrical power was supplied by a 28-volt DC system, powered by two engine driven starter-generators. A 24-volt storage battery served as a stand-by, supplying power to part of the system when the generators were inoperative or when generator output was insufficient. Alternating current was supplied to the system by one main single-phase inverter with a three-phase adapter and a stand-by three-phase inverter.

ELECTRICAL POWER DISTRIBUTION: Power distribution was made through two busses, a battery bus and a main bus. Both busses were energized through bus tie-in relays when either one or both generators or an external source was powering the system. The battery, supplementing the generators, provided power for the battery bus alone, and completely powered this bus when no other power source was in use. All equipment essential to flight operated from the battery bus. The main bus, energized entirely by one or both generators, supplied power to nonessential equipment requiring heavier current than that supplied by the battery. The starter operated from external power only.

If the main inverter, energized by the main bus, became inoperative, the stand-by inverter which operated from the battery bus was automatically connected to the essential portion of the AC load. The essential AC load included the attitude gyro, the fuel and oil pressure indicators, the fuel quantity gage, and the gun-firing power transformer.

EXTERNAL POWER: Two external power receptacles were located aft of the main wheel well. The external power source was connected to the number "1" receptacle to make power available to both busses. If the number "2" receptacle was connected alone, power was supplied only to the main bus. Both receptacles were used for engine starting.

HYDRAULIC SYSTEMS: Hydraulic power was supplied by two systems, a constant-pressure utility system and an open center boost system. Fluid for both systems were stored in a single reservoir which was divided into two sections. Each system had a separate pump that received fluid from one section of the reservoir. The hydraulic fluid was MIL-O-5606.

The utility system was powered by an engine-driven, variable-output pump providing constant pressure of approximately 3,000 psi to operate the landing gear, nose wheel steering, speed brakes, and wheel brakes. An accumulator was included in the brake system for emergency use.

The open-center boost system was a non-pressurized system having no means of pressure storage. A separate engine-driven, constant volume pump circulated fluid through the system without building up pressure until a control valve was moved to an operating position. Then fluid circulation was restricted at the affected control valve to build up pressure required to perform the desired operation. This system supplied pressure for aileron and elevator control boost systems.

A hydraulic emergency boost supply selector was located on the left console forward of the throttle. If the boost pump failed, the selector was moved from "NORM." to "EMERG." to direct utility system pressure to the aileron and elevator boost system.

PRIMARY FLIGHT CONTROLS: The primary flight controls were conventionally operated, however, the open-center hydraulic system supplied boost assistance to the ailerons and elevators, reducing the amount of force required for their movement. Conventional rudder and aileron trim tabs were provided, but, instead of conventional elevator trim, the complete horizontal stabilizer was adjustable. An electrically actuated trim tab was provided on the left aileron.

The aircraft was equipped with a standard B8 Control Grip. The "coolie hat" (the knurled switch on the control stick) controlled the horizontal stabilizer adjustment and aileron trim. A nose wheel steering switch was mounted on the control stick in addition to a combination gun trigger and gun camera switch, a bomb and rocket release switch, and a radar target reject switch.

The rudder pedals were hinged to fold back, enabling the pilot to use their padded forward surfaces as footrests.

Conventional pedal adjustment was accomplished by means of a handle forward of the pedestal.

PRIMARY FLIGHT CONTROL SURFACE BOOST: To reduce stick forces in flight, the open-center hydraulic system supplied boost pressure for movement of the ailerons and elevators. Hydraulic pressure was supplied by the engine-driven hydraulic pump, and normally, the system was operative at all times when the engine was running. Should the system fail, the stick forces would be considerably increased, but the airplane was still controllable. In such an emergency, if the malfunction was caused by failure of the hydraulic system, electrically actuated aileron and elevator boost by-pass valves automatically opened, reducing stick forces. If the by-pass valves failed to open, stick forces would become excessively high. However, the valves could be immediately opened by means of a boost by-pass switch on the emergency control panel.

PITCH CONTROL SYSTEM: The conventional pitch control consisted of hydraulic operated elevators and movable horizontal stabilizer. The open-center hydraulic system supplied boost assistance to the elevators, reducing the amount of force required for their movement.

The angle of incidence of the horizontal stabilizer could be varied between +3 degrees and -9 degrees by means of a normal or an emergency control. Stabilizer position was shown on an indicator on the instrument panel.

A four-position emergency horizontal stabilizer switch was located on the emergency control panel. When the emergency switch was at "NORMAL," stabilizer position was adjusted by the normal stabilizer switch on the control stick grip. If the normal stabilizer switch failed, the stabilizer was operated by moving the emergency stabilizer switch to either of the spring-loaded positions, "NOSE UP" or "NOSE DOWN." When the center, "OFF", position was selected, both normal and emergency switches were disconnected.

ROLL CONTROL SYSTEM: The conventional roll control consisted of hydraulic operated ailerons. The open-center hydraulic system supplied boost assistance to the ailerons, reducing the amount of force required for their movement.

An electrically actuated trim tab on the left aileron was normally adjusted by the coolie hat on the control stick. Emergency operation of the aileron trim tab was provided by an alternate aileron trim tab switch on the emergency control panel. With the alternate trim tab switch at "NORMAL STICK GRIP", the aileron trim tab was controlled by the normal aileron trim tab switch. If the normal aileron trim tab switch failed, the alternate trim tab switch was moved to either of the spring-loaded positions, "RIGHT" or "LEFT" to control the aileron trim tab. Moving the alternate aileron trim tab switch from the "NORMAL STICK GRIP" position also cut off electrical power to the normal horizontal stabilizer switch. Subsequent movement of the horizontal stabilizer needed to be accomplished by means of the emergency switch.

YAW CONTROL SYSTEM: The conventional yaw control consisted of a non-boosted hydraulic operated rudder. An electrically actuated rudder trim tab was controlled by a spring-loaded switch on the left aft console. The tab was set to the neutral position by holding the switch at "NOSE RIGHT" or "NOSE LEFT".

SURFACE CONTROL LOCK: The throttle, control stick, and rudder pedals could be locked by means of a lock handle on the armament panel below the instrument panel.

SECONDARY FLIGHT CONTROLS:
Wing Slats: Two wing slats extended from the fuselage to the wing tip along the leading edge of each wing panel. Aerodynamic forces acting upon the slats caused them to open and close automatically, depending upon the airspeed, G-load, and attitude of the airplane. When they opened, the slats move forward along a curved track, forming a slot in the wing leading edge. This automatic extension of the slats changed the airflow over the wing upper surface and increased lift, resulting in lower stalling speeds. At higher speeds, in unaccelerated flight, the slats automatically close to provide minimum drag for maximum performance in flight. No locks were provided for the slats.

Above, YF-93 flaps down full 38°. (Craig Kaston collection) Bottom, YF-93 with wing slats extended. (Craig Kaston collection)

Flaps: Electrically operated, slotted type wing flaps extended from the aileron to the fuselage on each wing panel. Actuators were installed at each flap and were interconnected by a flexible shaft. No separate emergency system was provided for operating the flaps, but the flexible shaft enabled one actuator to operate both flaps should the electrical power to the other actuator fail. A flap position indicator calibrated in degrees was located on the left console.

The flap control handle was located on the left side of the cockpit. Detents were provided at three positions: "UP", "DOWN" and "OFF". To operate the flaps, the handle was moved to the" UP" or "DOWN" position until the desired setting was reached, and returned to "OFF" to disconnect the actuator electrical circuits.

Speed Brakes: Two hydraulically operated speed brakes were installed on the underside of the fuselage, and extended down into the airstream when opened. The speed brakes were held open by hydraulic pressure, and held closed by mechanical locks. No emergency means was provided for opening the speed brakes, but if they were opened at a time of either an electrical or hydraulic failure, could be closed by using the emergency speed brake control.

A serrated rotary switch on top of the power control unit controlled the speed

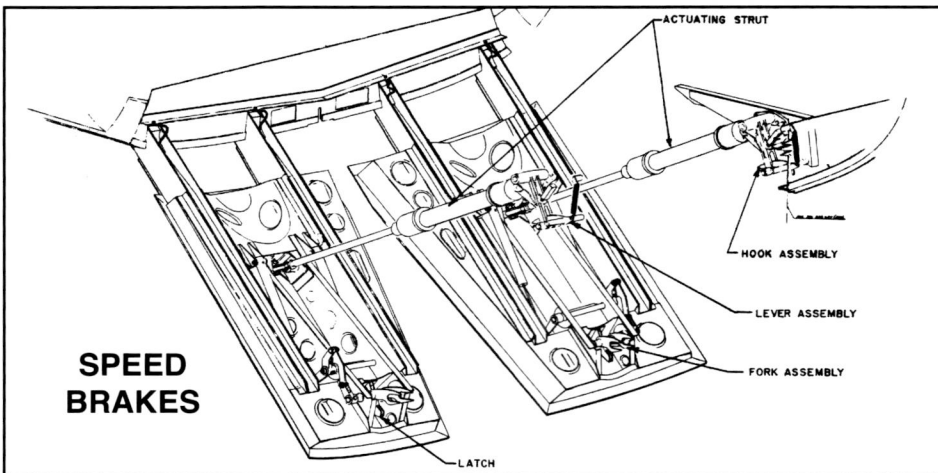

SPEED BRAKES

ACTUATING STRUT

HOOK ASSEMBLY

LEVER ASSEMBLY

FORK ASSEMBLY

LATCH

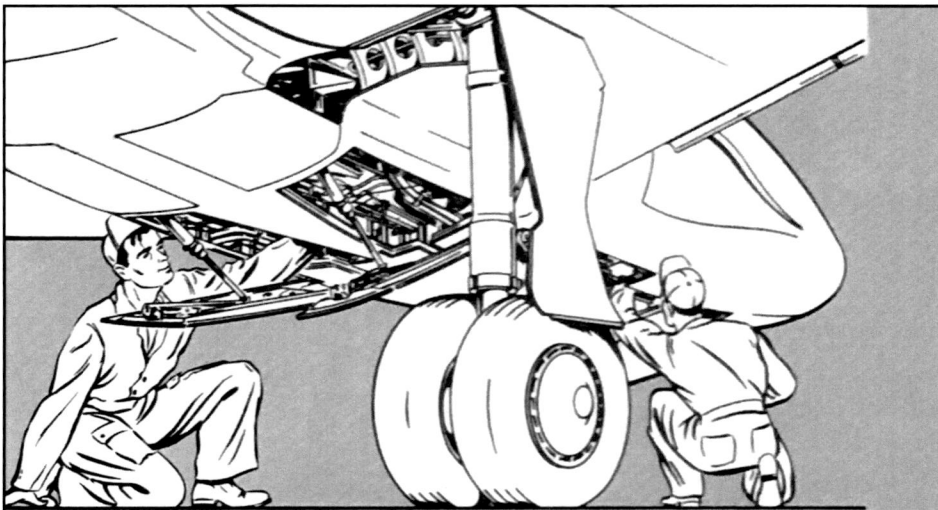

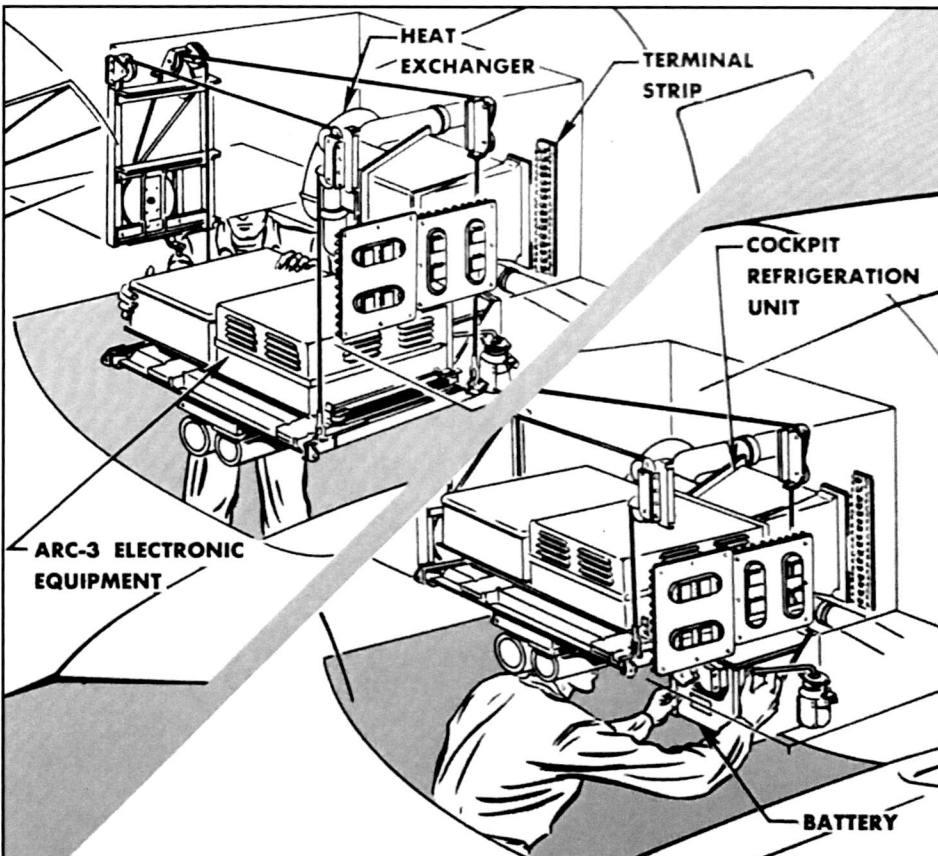

HEAT EXCHANGER

TERMINAL STRIP

COCKPIT REFRIGERATION UNIT

ARC-3 ELECTRONIC EQUIPMENT

BATTERY

brake hydraulic control valve. The switch had two spring-loaded positions, "IN" and "OUT" and maintained an off position which was indicated by a white mark on the switch guide.

To provide a means of closing the speed brakes when normal operation failed, an emergency speed brake control was installed just outboard of the throttle. When moved from "NORMAL" to "EMERG" the control mechanically opened a dump valve, relieving hydraulic pressure from the speed brake actuating cylinders. Air loads then closed the brakes.

LANDING GEAR: The heavier weight of the YF-93A dictated a major change in the landing gear configuration from the F-86 it was derived from. This increased weight necessitated a dual-wheel main landing gear and increased braking power.

The landing gear and wheel fairing doors were hydraulically actuated and electrically controlled and sequenced. The main gear retracted inboard into the wing panels and fuselage. The nose gear retracted forward into the nose. Incorporated in the nose gear assembly was a hydraulic steering unit which acted as a conventional shimmy damper when the steering mechanism was not engaged. Hydraulic actuated brakes were provided for the main wheels.

The landing gear emergency up-lock release crank, located on the right console, was used when either electrical or hydraulic failure prevented normal lowering of the landing gear. Turning the crank counterclockwise would mechanically release the landing gear up-locks. In the event of electrical failure, the gear could be lowered by positioning the landing gear control lever to "DOWN" and releasing the up-locks by turning the emergency

Above left, with the speed brakes open, a large maintenance area was exposed through which the hydraulic system components could be reached. At left, a large equipment bay could be accessed through the wheel wells. This included the battery, cockpit refrigeration unit, electrical terminal strip, and heat exchanger. The ARC-3 VHF equipment was also accessed by lowering an elevator. (all NAA Boeing via Mike Lombardi)

release crank counterclockwise. The gear would then be lowered normally by hydraulic pressure. In the event of hydraulic failure, the landing gear control handle could be placed in the "DOWN" position, the emergency release crank turned counterclockwise, and the gear would fall by its own weight. Yawing the airplane would lock the gear in the down position.

Hydraulic pressure was supplied to the nose gear steering unit through a shutoff valve actuated by a steering switch button on the control stick grip. When the button was depressed, with the nose wheel on the ground and the shock strut partially compressed, the nose wheel could be turned approximately 27 degrees either side of center by rudder pedal action. Before the steering mechanism could be engaged, the rudder pedals had to be coordinated with the nose wheel position.

Power brakes on the main wheels were operated by toe pedals with pressure supplied from the utility system. An accumulator provided emergency operating pressure in case the utility system pressure was not available. The brakes could be locked for parking by means of a parking brake handle located on the center pedestal.

At right, cockpit access was gained by using a step in the lowered ammo can door, then one on the intake lip and finally a bar lowered from the upper intake lip. Good view of the left side of the nose gear. (Craig Kaston collection) Below, the YF-93's forward nose gear door and inboard main gear doors were normally closed except during gear lowering and retracting or for maintenance as seen here. (Mark Aldrich collection)

RIGHT MAIN GEAR

NOSE GEAR RIGHT SIDE

Above, the outer YF-93 windshield was made of two panels forming a V. It was prone to reflection and distortion when landing. (William Simone collection)

CANOPY MECHANISMS

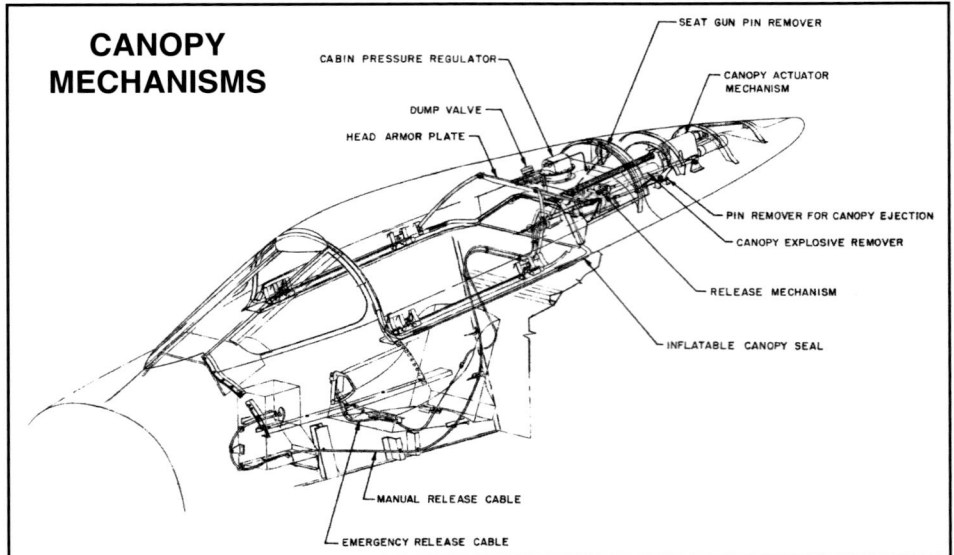

CANOPY AND WINDSHIELD: Like its predecessor, the YF-93A was equipped with a large bubble canopy and a three piece windshield. The side panels were curved while the center section was made of two flat sections forming a V. This center section consisted of an inner panel of armor glass and an outer windshield glass panel. Like the F-86, the canopy slid aft on two tracks. It was designed to be opened in flight up to a speed of approximately 215 KIAS.

The electrically operated bubble canopy was controlled from either inside or outside the airplane. Externally there were two spring-loaded push-button switches located on each side of the fuselage directly behind the engine air ducts. The canopy was opened or closed by holding in the respective push button. Emergency release of the canopy in flight was accomplished by means of a canopy ejection gun which fired the canopy off the airplane.

An inflatable canopy seal was provided which sealed the canopy in the closed position. Pressure for inflation of the seal was provided by engine compressor air and was automatically controlled by a pressure regulator. The seal became inflated whenever the canopy was fully closed. When any of the canopy switch buttons were actuated, the seal was automatically deflated to allow the canopy to move. The seal was also automatically deflated before canopy ejection.

The canopy ejection gun was fired when the right handgrip on the seat was pulled full up in preparation for seat ejection. When the canopy was ejected in flight, a seat ejection lock pin that prevented the seat ejection until after the canopy left the airplane was pulled from the seat catapult firing mechanism.

An internal manual handle was provided on the right side of the canopy bow for pulling the canopy open in the event it could not be opened electrically. The declutch handle on the bottom of the center pedestal had to be held out while the canopy was being pulled open manually. It was for ground use only and, when pulled, disengaged the canopy from the drive shaft so it could be moved manually. The canopy declutch handle did not release the canopy in flight.

An external canopy emergency release handle could be reached through an access door on the right side of the fuselage below the canopy frame. The external release did not fire the canopy remover gun, but merely released the canopy so it could be moved manually.

At left and below, the YF-93 ejection seat was similar to the early F-86A, but more rugged. (NAA/Boeing via Mike Lombardi)

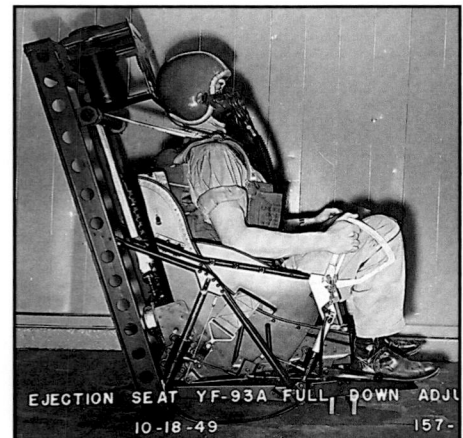

EJECTION SEAT: An ejection seat, similar to that of an early F-86A, was provided which would catapult the pilot clear of the tail surfaces. The pilot's manual states that the seat was good for any speed, but there is no envelope or test results to verify this. A catapult mounted aft of the seat supplied the propelling force to eject the seat and pilot from the cockpit. Armrests and footrests on the seat were fixed, but the handgrips provided were hinged to pull into an up position for ejection. When the seat was ejected, the anti-G suit, oxygen hose, microphone and headset connections automatically disconnected at a single fitting attached to the seat between the footrests

The ejection seat operation was similar to that of the early F-86A. The seat catapult trigger lever, located beneath the folding handgrip at the forward end of the right armrest, was protected by a guard and safety wire. As the right handgrip was pulled up in preparation for ejection, the safety wire was broken and the trigger was raised out of the guard. At its full up position, the canopy was released and the handgrip locks, with the trigger lever were now within reach of the fingers. Squeezing the trigger fired the seat catapult. The seat ejection lock pin in the seat catapult firing mechanism rendered the trigger lever ineffective until after the canopy was ejected.

A conventional control for adjusting the seat elevation was provided on the right forward corner of the seat. There was no forward or aft adjustment. Pulling the handle up released the seat for adjustment, and the seat could be raised when the pilot lifted his weight from it. The weight of the seat was counterbalanced to permit ease of operation.

ASSIST TAKE-OFF UNITS (ATO/JATO): Provisions were made on the underside of the fuselage for six ATO/JATO units. Each unit supplied 1,000 pounds of thrust for 14 seconds. An ATO/JATO firing switch button on the instrument panel controlled the firing of the ATO/JATO units. The throttle had to be fully advanced before firing was possible. The units were released by moving the ATO/JATO release switch adjacent to the firing switch from the guarded off position "to RELEASE.

COCKPIT HEATING, VENTILATION, AND PRESSURIZATION: Air for heating, cooling, and pressurizing the cockpit was normally supplied by the engine compressor. In an emergency, ram air was supplied from an intake duct in the fuselage nose. Normal airflow to the cockpit was distributed by two systems, a main and an auxiliary. For the main system, hot air from the compressor was partially diverted through a cooling unit by means of a mixing valve which was automatically regulated by an automatic temperature control system. This air entered the cockpit through outlets at the pilot's feet and at defrosting outlets at the windshield, armor glass, and canopy. The auxiliary system supplied air for canopy defrosting when the main system air became inadequate. A defrost heater was provided for heating the main and auxiliary system defrost air, if necessary. The auxiliary air could also be diverted through an anti-ice heater to a windshield anti-ice outlet between the armor glass and the outer windshield panel. The emergency ram air was directed to the windshield, armor glass, and canopy outlets only. This air could enter the cockpit directly from the ram air

Above, JATO/ATO was needed for takeoffs on hot days and heavy weights. (Kaston collection) Below, high-speed taxi with six JATO bottles attached. (Kaston collection) Bottom, provisions were made for six JATO units. Each unit supplied 1,000 lbs of thrust for 14 seconds. (William Simone collection)

intake, or first be heated by the defrost heater.

A pressure regulator automatically maintained

YF-93A COCKPIT - FORWARD VIEW

cabin pressure equivalent to a 10,000-foot altitude from 10,000 feet to 18,000 feet actual altitude. Above that, the regulator maintained a 2.75 psi pressure differential between cockpit and outside air. However, no cockpit pressurization was provided with the emergency ram air system.

ANTI-G SUIT PROVISIONS: An air pressure outlet connection on the front of the pilot's seat provided an attachment of the air pressure intake tube of the pilot's anti-G suit. Air pressure for inflation of the anti-G suit bladders was supplied from the engine compressor through a pressure regulating valve located on the left console, which started functioning at acceleration above approximately 1.75G causing the valve to open, inflating the anti-G suit. As acceleration increased, suit pressure increased proportionally. The amount of increase in pressure depended on the setting of the valve, which could be turned to either "HI" or "LO". When acceleration decreased, suit pressure decreased. A button on top of the valve could be manually depressed to inflate the suit momentarily when desired, lessening fatigue during prolonged flight. The author can incontrovertibly state that this early G-suit was pure torture.

LIGHTING EQUIPMENT
Exterior Position Lights and Fuselage Lights: The position lights on the wing tips and tail were controlled by a selector switch and a dimmer switch on the left instrument subpanel. When positioned at either "STEADY" or "FLASH," the selector switch turned the lights on. Desired brilliancy of the lights could be selected by placing the dimmer switch at "BRIGHT" or "DIM".

The fuselage lights, one on top and one on the bottom of the fuselage, each contain one small and one large lamp. When the fuselage light switch on the left instrument subpanel was positioned at "BRIGHT" or "DIM", the small lamps were illuminated and burn steadily. The large lamps were controlled only by a master code switch and a code selector, and were used only for automatic flashing of selected code letters.

A master code switch and a code selector on the left instrument subpanel controlled automatic code flashing of the fuselage lights and position lights. The master code switch controls provided the choice of twelve letters for flashing. With the master code switch "ON" and code selector turned to the desired letter, the large fuselage lamps automatically flashed the selected letter in Morse code. The position lights could also be flashed.

A code indicator light, on the left instrument subpanel, flashed simultaneously with the large lamps in the fuselage lights, indicating that the selected letter was being flashed.

Landing and Taxi Lights: Two retractable landing lights were located in the fuselage nose just forward of the nose wheel door, and were controlled by a switch on the left instrument subpanel.

A taxi light was mounted on the nose gear and was controlled by a switch mounted on the instrument subpanel. The taxi light also illuminated when the landing light switch was on and the weight of the airplane was on the gear.

Interior Lighting: Instrument panel lighting was supplied by two fixed fluorescent lights, one on each side of the cockpit. The instrument and console lights were lit by three adjustable red lights while the switch panels were illuminated indirectly. An extension light for general cockpit illumination was mounted on the right side of the cockpit.

ENGINE FIRE DETECTOR SYSTEM: Warning of an engine fire was given by indicator lights mounted on the engine control panel. Two lights were provided, a red light to indicate fire in the forward engine compartment and an amber light to indicate overheat or fire in the aft engine compartment. A stainless steel firewall divided the engine compartment at a point immediately aft of the compressor. The forward engine compartment included the compressor and accessory section. The aft engine compartment included the combustion chambers and tail pipe.

AUTOMATIC PILOT: The YF-93A included full up systems that would be required to perform it mission. One such system installed was an electrically operated automatic pilot. Direct current was supplied by the engine-driven generators and alternating current was supplied by the main inverter. Should the main inverter or generators fail, the auto-pilot was inoperative. It was connected to the slaved gyro magnetic compass and could be used in conjunction with the instrument landing equipment to guide the airplane during an instrument approach. Most of the automatic pilot controls and indicators were easily accessible being located on the right console.

INSTRUMENT PANEL LEGEND:

1.) Emergency Brake Handle
2.) Inverter Warning Lights
3.) Landing Gear Emergency-Up Switch
4.) Radio Compass Indicator (AN/ARN-6)
5.) Machmeter
6.) Accelerometer
7.) Airspeed Indicator
8.) Horizontal Stabilizer Position Indicator
9.) Clock
10.) Slaved Gyro Magnetic Compass
11.) Voltage Selector Switch
12.) Turn-and-Bank Indicator
13.) Generator Load Meters
14.) Rate-of-Climb Indicator
15.) Oil Temperature Indicator
16.) Altitude Gyro
17.) Oil Pressure Indicator
18.) Voltmeter
19.) Tachometer
20.) Cockpit Air Temperature Gage
21.) Exhaust Temperature Indicator
22.) Overheat Warning Test Switch
23.) Forward Engine Compartment Fire
      Indicator Light
24.) Stand-By Compass
25.) Aft Engine Comp. Overheat Light
26.) Aft CG Warning Light
27.) Generator Switches
28.) Fuel Tank Damage Control Switch
29.) Fuel CG Control Switch
30.) Fuel Regulator Selector Switch
31.) Fuel Pump Test Switch
32.) Emergency Fuel Regulator Ind. Light
33.) Ground Start Switch
34.) Engine Master Switch
35.) Battery Switch
36.) Fuel Pressure Indicator
37.) Cabin Altimeter
38.) Fuel Flowmeter and Counter
39.) Fuel Quantity Gage
40.) Generator Overvoltage Warning Lights
41.) Rudder Pedal Adjustment Handle
42.) Bomb-Target Wind Control
43.) Canopy Declutch Handle
44.) Fragmentation Bomb Control Panel
45.) Rocket Setting Unit
46.) Chemical Tank Selector Switch
47.) Surface Control Lock Handle
48.) Rocket Control Panel
49.) Demolition Bomb Control Panel
50.) Filament Selector Switches
51.) Gun Control Panel
52.) Parking Brake Handle
53.) Rudder and Aileron Trim-Tab-in-Neutral
      Light
54.) Cross-Pointer Indicator
55.) Altimeter
56.) Landing Gear Position Indicators
57.) Landing Gear Control Handle
58.) Taxi Light Switch
59.) Landing Light Switch
60.) Master Code Switch
61.) Code Selector
62.) Code Indicator Light
63.) Position Light Selector Switch
64.) Position Light Dimmer Switch
65.) ATO/JATO Firing Switch
66.) ATO/JATO Release Switch
67.) Pilot Heater Switch
68.) Inverter Control Switch

PILOT'S LEFT-HAND CONSOLE:

1.) Circuit Breaker Panel
2.) Heat and Vent Control Panel

3.) Temperature Control Rheostat
4.) Console Lights
5.) Canopy Air Outlet
6.) Fluorescent Light
7.) Normal Speed Brake Control
8.) Bomb and Rocket Jettison Switch
9.) Emergency Horizontal Stabilizer Switch
10.) Air Start Switch
11.) Alternate Aileron Trim Tab Switch
12.) Control Surface Boost By-Pass Switch
13.) Instrument Light
14.) Canopy Push-Button Switches
15.) Instrument Subpanel
16.) Emergency Control Panel
17.) Hydraulic Emergency Boost Supply
18.) Flap Position Indicator
19.) Oxygen Flow Indicator

20.) Oxygen Pressure Gage
21.) Oxygen Regulator
22.) Gyro Caging Button
23.) Emergency Speed Brake Control
24.) Power Control Friction Wheel
25.) Microphone Switch
26.) Left Seat Handgrip
27.) Rudder Trim Tab Switch
28.) Flap Control Handle
29.) Power Control
30.) Windshield Anti-Ice Lever
31.) Defrost Heater Switch
32.) Canopy Air Outlet Control Lever
33.) Windshield and Canopy Air Lever
34.) Cockpit Pressure Switch
35.) Cockpit Temperature Control Switch
36.) Anti-G Suit Pressure Valve

PILOT'S LEFT-HAND CONSOLE

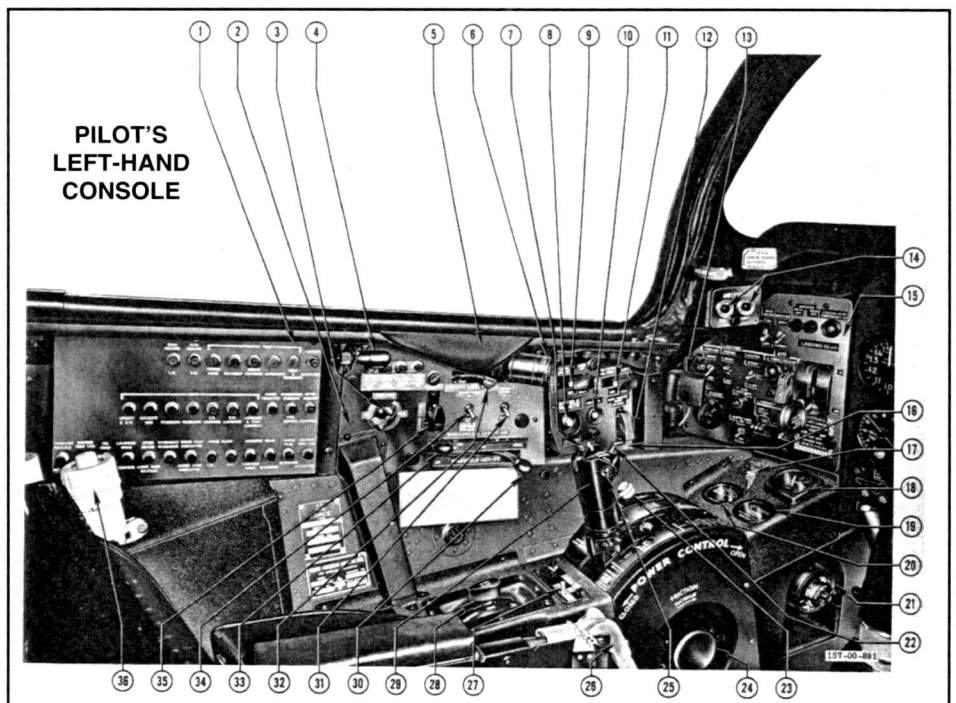

21

YF-93A COCKPIT LEFT SIDE

157-30-4C

YF-93A COCKPIT - RIGHT SIDE

KPIT LEFT

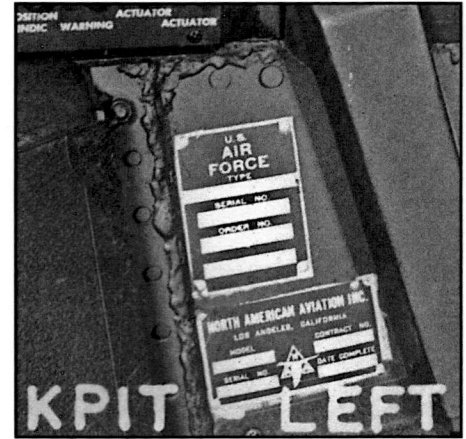

At left, pilot's left-hand console. (NAA/Boeing) Middle left, pilot's right-hand console. (NAA/Boeing via Mike Lombardi) Above, YF-93 S/N 48-318 Data Plate. (William Simone collection) Bottom left, pilot's right-hand console drawing. (William Simone collection)

PILOT'S RIGHT-HAND CONSOLE:
1.) Engine Control Panel
2.) Control Stick
3.) Radio Compass Panel (AN/ARN-6)
4.) Fluorescent Light Control Rheostat
5.) Instrument Light Control Rheostat
6.) Console Light Switch
7.) Switch Panel Light Control Rheostat
8.) Instrument Light
9.) Automatic Pilot Engaging Handle
10.) Boost Pressure Gage
11.) Stand-By Compass Light Switch
12.) Console Light
13.) Fluorescent Light
14.) Automatic pilot Turn Knob
15.) Automatic Pilot Turn Indicators
16.) Automatic Pilot Climb Control Wheel
17.) Automatic Pilot Indicator Light
18.) Stand-By Compass Correction Card
19.) Canopy Air Outlet Control Lever
20.) Canopy Air Outlet
21.) Instrument Approach Control Panel
22.) Console Light
23.) Automatic Approach Control Selector
24.) Radar Ranging Control Panel
    (AN/APG-30)
25.) Command Radio Control Panel
    (AN/ARC-3)
26.) Automatic Pilot Altitude Control
27.) Automatic Pilot Aileron Trim Control
28.) Main Automatic Pilot Switch
29.) Automatic Pilot Control Central
30.) Automatic Pilot Glide Control Wheel
31.) Relief Tube
32.) Landing Gear Emergency Up-Lock
    Realease Indicator
33.) Landing Gear Emergency Up-Lock
    Release Crank
34.) Normal Horizontal Stabilizer/Aileron
    Trim Tab Switch
35.) Bomb/Rocket Release Switch
36.) Radar Target Reject Switch
37.) Nose Wheel Steering Switch
38.) Surface Control Lock Bolt
39.) Gun Trigger and Gun Camera Switch
40.) Circuit Breaker Panel

WEAPON SYSTEMS:

Gun Sight: The YF-93A was equipped with a Type A-1B sight head, located above the instrument panel shroud. It automatically computed leads as a gun, bomb, or rocket sight. The sight reticle image, consisting of a circle and central dot, was reflected on the bullet-resistant windshield glass. The sight was entirely automatic, requiring only that the center dot be kept on the target and the target tracked smoothly. The sight was operable as a gun sight from sea level to 40,000 feet, and as a bomb sight from sea level to 10,000 feet. For gunnery operation, an AN/APG-30 radar ranging unit was used with the sight, however, on overland targets below 5000 feet, radar ranging was impossible and manual ranging was required. Bombs could be released automatically at the proper release point through operation of the sight.

The AN/APG-30 was an X-Band lightweight, airborne, radar fire control system for range-only measurement. The antenna was a simple horn feed installed in the nose of the aircraft. The radar continuously supplied target range information to a range servomechanism for operation and control of the Type A-1B lead-computing gunsight system. It was used on the B-45, B-57, F-4E, F-8A, F-84E, F-86A (final blocks only), F-86E/F, F-100, FJ-2, and F2H-2.

Gunnery Equipment: A bank of three 20 mm guns was mounted on each side of the fuselage in the nose of the airplane. Two hundred and twenty-five rounds of ammunition could be carried for each gun. All guns were charged in flight, thus providing a means of ejecting faulty shells in the event of a misfire. Pneumatic gun chargers were installed on each gun and were controlled by a single gun charger button on the gun control panel on the center pedestal. All guns were charged simultaneously. A camera mounted in the right wing leading edge was operated automatically when guns or rockets were fired, or could be operated separately.

At right, three 20mm guns were mounted on each side of the fuselage as seen here in the mock-up on 21 September 1948. 225 rounds of ammunition could be carried for each gun in the ammo cans beneath them. (NAA/Boeing via Mark Lombardi)

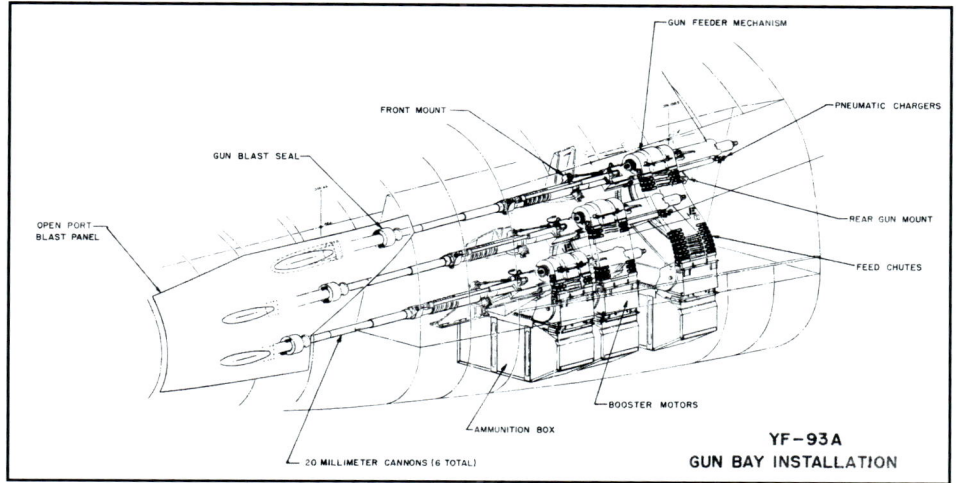

YF-93A
GUN BAY INSTALLATION

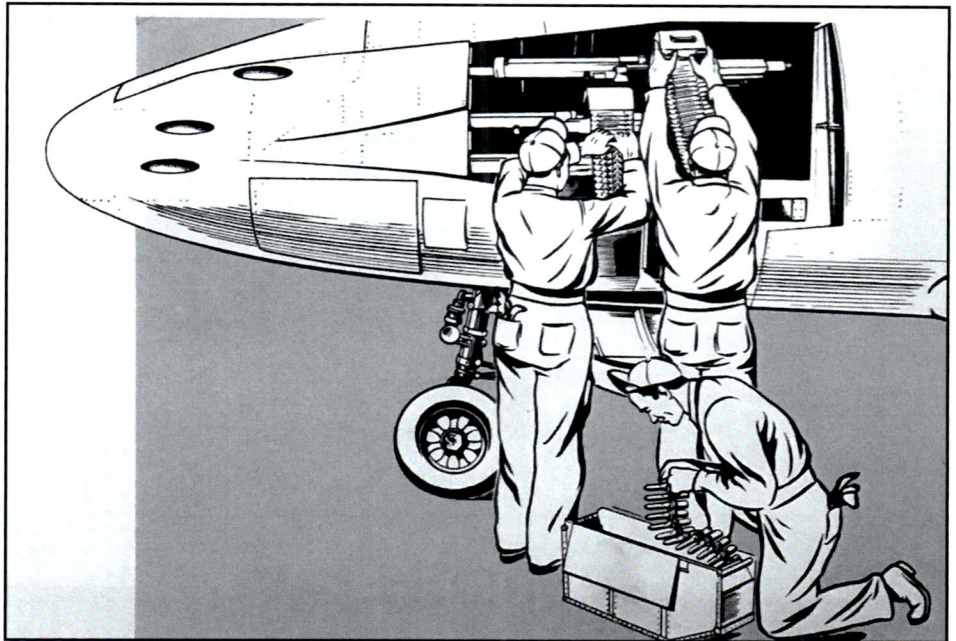

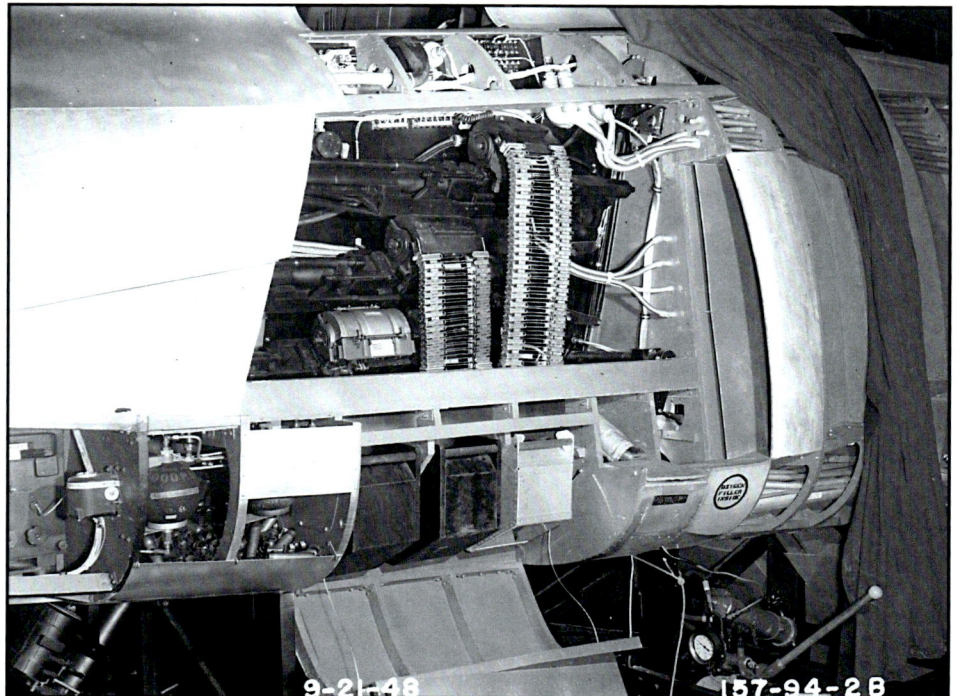

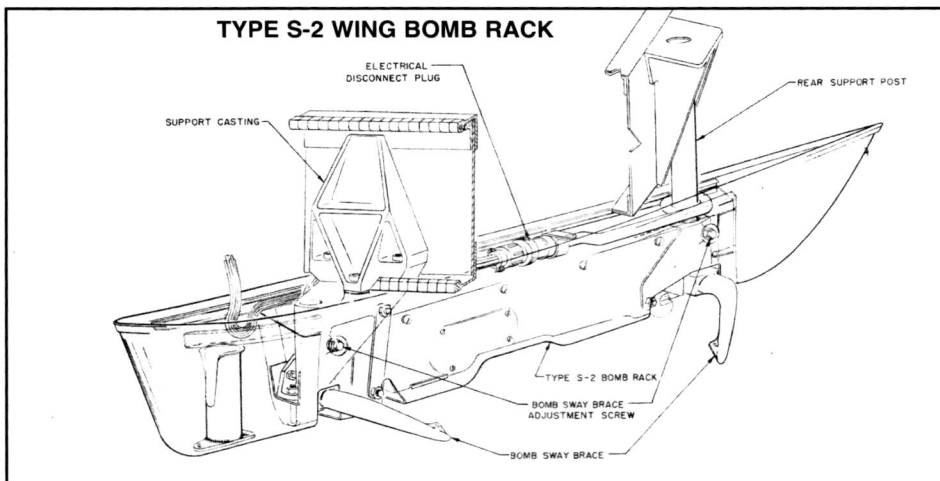

TYPE S-2 WING BOMB RACK

ELECTRICAL DISCONNECT PLUG

SUPPORT CASTING

REAR SUPPORT POST

TYPE S-2 BOMB RACK

BOMB SWAY BRACE ADJUSTMENT SCREW

BOMB SWAY BRACE

The ammunition compartment could be heated when necessary to maintain suitable temperature for firing. When the system was turned on, hot air was extracted from the supply duct for the cockpit heating system and routed to both ammunition compartments. The air supplied to the ammunition compartments was automatically controlled to maintain the desired ammunition temperature range.

Below, ship two showing the gun and rocket installations. (Craig Kaston collection) Bottom, close-up of 8 5" rockets under the right wing. (William Simione collection)

Bombing Equipment: A type S-2 bomb rack could be mounted under each outer wing panel to carry single bombs from 100 to 1,000 pounds, bomb clusters up to 500 pounds, or para-fragmentation bomb racks and bombs. The A-1B sight was used for bomb sighting, and bombs were normally released by means of a bomb-rocket release switch on top of the control stick grip. In addition, chemical tanks could be carried.

A Type M10 chemical tank could be carried on each bomb rack. The M10 smoke tank, also known as Smoke Curtain Installation, was an aircraft under-wing tank used by the United States Army Air Forces to lay smoke screens or dispense chemical weapons such as tear gas. The tanks held a maximum of 30 US gallons, and weighed, when full, 588 pounds and could lay a smoke screen about 2,000 feet long. Tank selection was provided by a switch on the center pedestal. After discharging chemicals (by means of the bombs/rockets release switch), the tanks could be dropped by operation of the bomb and rocket jettison switch or the normal bomb release system.

Rockets: Eight rockets could be carried under each wing on four rocket launchers, each holding two rockets. It was also proposed that six more could be mounted on the plane's belly in pairs. The A-1B sight was used for aiming rockets, and rockets were fired by depressing the bomb/rocket release switch on the control stick grip. The camera operated automatically when rockets were fired. A rocket projector release control was mounted on the left rear console.

For rocket firing, the rocket setting unit on the armament control panel was used to provide a depression angle correction for the type of rocket to be fired and the intended dive angle of the attack. Settings were provided for three types of rockets: 5 HVAR, 3.5 AR, and 5 AR. At each of the three positions were two detents marked "S" and "N" for setting the intended dive angle. For attacks between zero and 40 degrees, the pilot would set the control at "N" (normal), and for attacks between 40 degrees and 60 degrees, the control would be set at "S" (steep). A rocket release selector on the rocket control panel had "OFF", "SINGLE," and "AUTO" positions. At "SINGLE", one rocket was fired with each depression of the bomb release switch. On "AUTO", all rockets were released in train with one depression of the release switch, provided the switch was depressed for approximately 2 seconds. Rockets could not be jettisoned while the airplane was on the ground, as the rocket jettison circuit was inoperative with weight on wheels. In the event of engine failure on takeoff, a rocket jettison switch on the rocket control panel permitted the rockets to be jettisoned by means of the bomb-rocket release switch on the stick grip.

ROCKET INSTALLATION (5 INCH HVAR) YF-93A # 318

24

SINGLE PLACE ALL-WEATHER FIGHTER DESIGN STUDY

The design study for a single place all-weather fighter was the basic arrangement of the YF-93 single place aircraft modified to utilize the AN/APG-33 search radar coupled to an A-1B computing sight, a retractable rocket launcher located on the lower belly in place of the six 20 mm guns, all weather provisions, additional internal fuel and an internal water-alcohol tank for added thrust during hot day, high altitude takeoffs. It was to be powered by a Pratt and Whitney J48-P-3 engine.

Provisions for all weather operations were made through the incorporation of de-icing equipment for all the leading edges, improved cockpit heating and air-conditioning, and the inclusion of equipment allowing instrument takeoffs and landings. The AN/APG-33 search radar would be modified for one-man operation permitting unrestricted use of the aircraft for night attacks or during poor visibility or cold weather conditions.

Firepower: The heart of the proposed aircraft was its new firepower, a retractable launcher carrying twenty-four 2.75-inch-high velocity folding-fin unguided rockets which provided maximum destruction force with a minimum weight and additional aerodynamic drag. The rockets could be fired in small groups or in a ripple salvo.

The launcher was normally retracted into the bottom of the fuselage and extended only during firing of the rockets, much like the F-86D being developed at the same time. This arrangement was particularly advantageous because the clean aerodynamic lines of the aircraft were in no way altered as when rockets are carried externally. Even through a firing sequence, the drag created was only momentary, for the maximum period of extension was no more than 1.5 seconds – extension, retraction and firing cycles each required 0.5 seconds. Through an intervalometer, small groups or the entire 24 rockets could be fired, the firing sequence being staggered between launch stations to avoid interference between the rocket fins.

Like the F-86D rocket pod system, it incorporated a means of quick detachment which allowed the fastest time for loading of the rockets. Normally the rockets would be loaded singly from the rear, however with the quick detachment feature, the launcher could be loaded beforehand and switched out between each mission.

AUGUST 1949 ALL-WEATHER ROCKET ARMED INTERCEPTER

Electronic and Radar Equipment: To attain the greatest degree of operation effectiveness, the proposed aircraft would be equipped with the AN/APG-33 radar, modified for single pilot operation. It was considered superior in range and accuracy to any of the equipment then installed in fighters. The advantageous feature of the AN/APG-33 radar was its ability to search over a much greater range.

Additional electronic equipment to be installed included:
AN/ARC-3 VHF Command Radio
AN/ARN-13 Marker Beacon
AN/ARN-6 Radio Compass
AN/ARN-5A Glide Path
RC-103 Localizer
AN/APX-6 IFF
C-2 Autopilot
A-1B Gyro Computing Sight

Fuel System: To achieve improved all-weather performance, the fuel system needed to be modified to incorporate an additional tank either side of the rocket launcher beneath the cockpit floor. Incorporated as a separate compartment in the fuel tank just above the main gear wheel wells was a 35-gallon water-alcohol tank for the water injection system.

The change from guns to rockets and the rearrangement of radio equipment permitted the installation of a pair of forward fuel cells which, with other modifications to the fuel system, increased the total internal self-sealing fuel tankage from 1,581 to 1,702 gallons.

Above, the F-93 all-weather fighter would have had the 24-shot 2.75" high velocity folding-fin unguided rocket tray seen here on an F-86D. (William Simone collection) Below, rocket tray extension mechanism. (NAA/Boeing via Mike Lombardi)

Anti-Icing and De-Icing Systems: All-weather operation of the aircraft was ensured by the use of heated wing and tail surfaces de-icing systems to be used in conjunction with a heated windshield anti-icing system. The surface de-icing

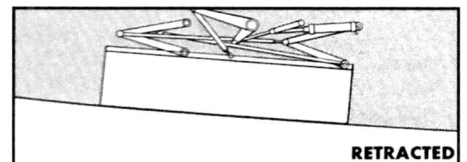

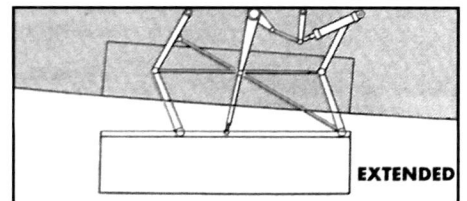

RETRACTED

EXTENDED

ALL-WEATHER ROCKET ARMED INTERCEPTOR
Electronic and Radar Layout

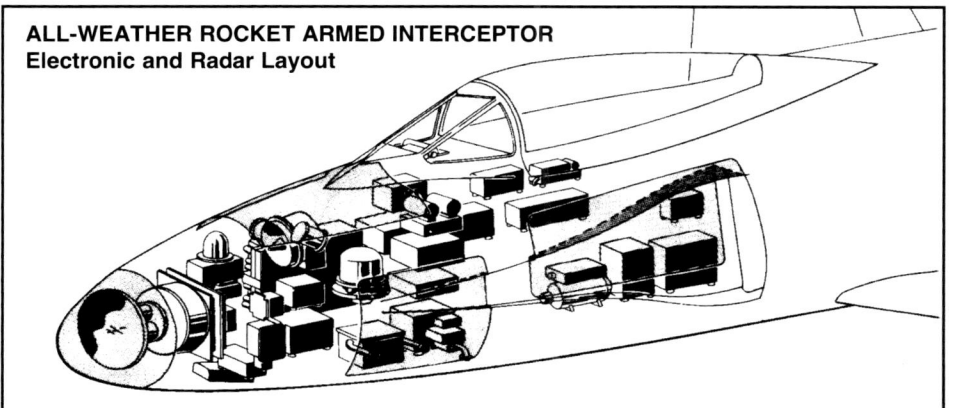

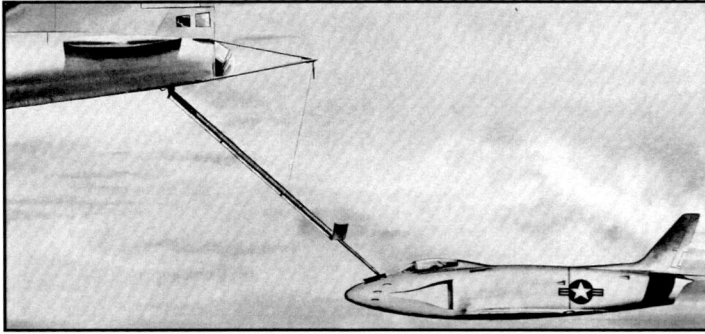

system consisted of electrical heating pads applied to the internal surfaces of the wing and tail leading edges, deriving energy from a 40 kva alternator mounted directly on the engine power takeoff drive pad. To reduce the electrical power required to a minimum and provide adequate protection of the aircraft, power would have been cycled to various sections of the wing and tail surfaces. Windshield anti-icing would be accomplished by means of hot air from the engine.

Performance and Range: It was predicted that the aircraft would have an allowable dive speed of 1.05 Mach and a maximum speed of 622 knots at sea level. The power available permitted a rate of climb that required only 3.58 minutes to 35,000 feet, nearly 10,000 feet/minute. With the increase in fuel, the combat radius was almost 700 nautical miles.

Performance Summary Single Place All-Weather Fighter Design Study with Pratt & Whitney J48-P-3 Engine

Take-Off Gross Weight	28,244 lbs
Fuel (All Internal)	1,702 gal
Water-Alcohol	35 gal
Take-Off Distance Over 50 ft Obstacle, No Wind, Flaps Down With Afterburner:	5,520 ft
AB & Water-Alcohol Injection	4,970 ft
Combat Radius	696 nm
Average Speed	453 kts
Combat Range	1,735 nm
Average Speed	451 kts
Combat Gross Weight	23,002 lbs
Max Speed at Sea Level:	
With Afterburner	622 kts
With Military Power	583 kts
Max Speed at 35,000 ft:	
With Afterburner	550 kts
With Military Power	513 kts
Time-To-Climb to 35,000 ft:	
With Afterburner Thrust	3.58 min
With Military Thrust	12.85 min
Service Ceiling:	
With Afterburner Thrust	47,400 ft
With Military Thrust	39,900 ft
Maneuverability at 40,000 ft at .85 Mach:	
Radius of Turn	20,650 ft
Rate of Turn	2.28 deg/sec
At 35,000 Feet:	
Radius of Turn	13,800 ft
Rate of Turn	3.44 deg/sec
Landing Gross Weight (10% Fuel Reserve)	18,024 Pounds
Stall Speed, Power Off, Dirty	107 kts
Landing Distance to Clear a 50 ft Obstacle – No Wind, Zero Thrust	3,950 ft

Notes: Standard Day Conditions, Pratt & Whitney J48-P-3 Engine
Afterburner plus Water-Alcohol:

Thrust	10,150 lbs
Afterburner Thrust	9,135 lbs
Military Trust	6,650 lbs

SINGLE PLACE ALL WEATHER FIGHTER DESIGN STUDY WITH WRIGHT TJ-14 ENGINE

In continued efforts to further improve the YF-93A, a preliminary study was conducted to evaluate performance gains available with the installation of an advanced, more powerful engine. The study resulted in a considerable gain in range, reduction in take-off ground roll, and increased ceiling and high altitude maneuverability. The engine studied was the Wright TJ-14, as denoted in Wright Aeronautical Corporation letters dated July 20 and October 9, 1949, and rated at 12,000 pounds thrust (unaugmented). The engine was an axial flow type of high performance per weight ratio and produced sufficient thrust at military power so that the added length and weight of an afterburner could be eliminated. The low specific fuel consumption figures for normal powers plus the elimination of the afterburner with its attendant high fuel consumption, resulted in a combat radius of 942 nautical miles with a reduction of fuel tankage to 1,445 gallons. This reduction in fuel tankage was necessary to maintain the combat weight load factors with the heavier engine and equipment. In addition to the increased radius, takeoff ground run was reduced approximately 1,000 feet, combat ceiling increased to 50,000 feet, and high-altitude maneuverability considerably increased. Space was provided for additional oxygen bottles during the extended missions.

Due to the higher airflow requirements of the TJ-14, the inlet duct area was increased from 450 to 746 square inches. This was done by refairing the ramp from a point 11 inches farther forward which in effect depresses the ramp inboard thus gaining the required area without disturbing the outer lip. The interior ducts were refaired into the single circular inlet for this type engine in place of the present plenum chamber-duct arrangement. Fuel tankage in this area needed to be revised because of the duct change.

Other than the TJ-14 engine and its related modifications, and inflight refueling provisions, all other systems remained unchanged. The fuselage disconnect joint (field break) was relocated forward to correspond to the mounting trunnion location of the TJ-14.

Wing, tail surfaces and leading edge anti-icing would be of the thermal type using hot air bleed from the engine compressor.

In keeping with the latest tactical thinking, an air-to-air refueling system was to be installed. This installation was based on the flying boom then being developed by the Boeing Aircraft Company and the Air Force in conjunction with North American Aviation studies for use in its fighter types. This arrangement consisted of the NAA fighter receptacle mounted in the top of the fuselage ahead of the windshield and with a fuel line running aft into the fuel tanks. The fuel system therefore would be changed to a single-point filling arrangement and easily adapted to single-point ground filling and defueling by the addition of a ground receptacle located on the side of the nose and teed into the fuel line. Retractable flush doors and suitable controls were installed to provide uninterrupted air flow over this area.

The radio and radar equipment would be rearranged because of the refueling receptacle installation and the change in the duct ramp. Since the two small forward fuel tanks were eliminated with the reduced fuel requirements, the displaced radio and radar equipment was now located in this space.

At top left, the TJ-14 engine proposal included in-flight refueling provisions. (Craig Kaston)

Above and below, two-place all-weather intercepter rocket tray armament of 24 2.75" high velocity, folding-fin, unguided rockets.

Performance Summary Single Place All-Weather Fighter Design Study with TJ-14 Engine and Inflight Refueling		
	Pratt & Whitney J48-P-3	**Wright TJ-14**
Take-Off Gross Weight:	27,713 lbs	27,852 lbs
Fuel	1,581 gal	1,445 gal
Take-Off Distance at Sea Level:		
Ground Run (no wind)	3,630 ft	2,645 ft
To Clear 50 Feet Obstacle	5,320 ft	3,395 ft
Combat Radius – No Inflight Refueling:	655 nm	942 nm
Average Cruising Speed	452 kts	489 kts
Total Mission Time	3.3 hrs	4.3 hrs
Combat Range – No Inflight Refueling:	1,657 nm	2,130 nm
Average Cruising Speed	451 kts	490 kts
Cruising Altitude	35,600 ft	44,100 ft
Combat Radius, 2 Inflight Refuelings:	2,474 nm	3,293 nm
Average Cruising Speed	453 kts	490 kts
Total Mission Time	11.3 hrs	13.9 hrs
Combat Range, 2 Inflight Refuelings:	5,305 nm	6,836 nm
Average Cruising Speed	453 kts	490 kts
Cruising Altitude	34,700 ft	43,600 ft
Performance Weight – No Refuelings:	22,965 lbs	23,002 lbs
Performance Altitude (over target)	34,600 ft	48,100 ft
Maximum Speed (over target):		
Afterburner Thrust	551 kts	----------
Military Thrust	515 kts	522 kts
Maximum Speed at Sea Level:		
Afterburner Thrust	622 kts	----------
Military Thrust	583 kts	605 kts
Rate-of-Climb at Sea Level:		
Afterburner Thrust	14,720 ft/min	----------
Military Thrust	5,070 ft/min	11,300 ft/min
Rate-of-Climb (over target):		
Afterburner Thrust	5,750 ft/min	----------
Military Thrust	1,150 ft/min	1,220 ft/min
Combat Ceiling (maximum thrust):	47,700 ft	50,200 ft
Service Ceiling:		
Maximum Thrust	47,400 ft	50,200 ft
Normal Thrust	36,600 ft	49,000 ft
Time-to-Climb, Sea Level TO 35,000 ft:		
Maximum Thrust	3.58	4.30
Maneuverability at .85 Mach:		
At 45,000 ft		
Radius-of-Turn	33,550 ft	26,920 ft
Rate-of-Turn	1.41 deg/sec	1.75 deg/sec
At 40,000 ft		
Radius-of-Turn	22,080 ft	16,500 ft
Rate-of-Turn	2.12 deg/sec	2.86 deg/sec

Notes: Standard Day Conditions.
Performance weight is the aircraft weight on arrival at the combat zone.
Performance altitude is the altitude corresponding to a 300 ft/min rate-of-climb with normal thrust at the performance weight.
Combat ceiling is the altitude corresponding to a 500 ft/min rate-of-climb.

	J48-P-3	**TJ-14**
Afterburner Thrust	9,135 lbs	----------
Military Trust	6,650 lbs	12,000 lbs

TWO PLACE ALL-WEATHER INTERCEPTOR

This design study was for a proposed two place all-weather interceptor capable of climbing rapidly and quickly locating and destroying enemy aircraft either in night or day and in all types of weather.

Like the basic F-93 it retained the J48 engine with afterburner but augmented with water injection (a J48-P-3 engine) thus permitting a high rate of climb.

The major changes consisted of additional cockpit and radar equipment, reduction of fuel load, the elimination of guns and ammunition, being replaced by a retractable rocket launcher located on the lower belly. Furthermore, additional cockpit air conditioning and heating was added to allow all weather operation.

External Modifications: The external modifications required to convert the

standard F-93A to a two-place all-weather interceptor were relatively minor. The cockpit enclosure was lengthened to accommodate the radar operator, and the fuselage nose was lengthened and refaired slightly to allow the new 20-inch radar antenna. Wings, empennage, landing gear and power plant installation were unchanged. The effect of these changes on the aerodynamics characteristics were deemed to be negligible.

To allow simultaneous entry by the crew into their cockpits and minimize ground time on scramble takeoffs, the aft sliding canopy was replaced by a large single-piece one that was hinged to open to the right side.

Cockpits: Flight and engine controls were located in the front cockpit only. The aft station contained all of the radar controls needed to complete the mission. Both stations were equipped with then advanced ejection seats with limited but sufficient operating envelope. The large one-piece canopy was ejected aft by an explosive charge.

Fuel System: The aircraft was to be equipped for a high-speed refueling via a single filler and featured a completely automatic sequencing fuel system requiring no attention from the pilot. Fuel was pumped to the engine and afterburner from the main fuselage tank, which received fuel automatically from all other tanks either by gravity or by transfer pumps.

The ability to refuel the aircraft completely through only a single filler, in conjunction with the rapid rearming feature of the aircraft, enabled the aircraft to perform additional interceptor missions in the shortest possible time. Fuel load was reduced to 775 gallons.

Water-Alcohol Injection System: The water-alcohol mixture was to be delivered to the engine by an air driven turbine pump from a 130-gallon bladder type cell. To prevent possible pump cavitation, the tank was pressurized with bleed air from the J48 engine compressor. In case of turbine pump failure, a simple means of dumping the water-alcohol mixture through the normal fuel system vent was provided so the tank could be emptied to reduce combat weight.

Armament: Like the single place all-weather fighter, it utilized a retractable rocket launcher located on the lower belly in place of the six 20 mm guns. The retractable launcher carried twenty-four 2.75-inch-high velocity folding-fin unguided rockets which provided maximum destruction force with a minimum weight or additional aerodynamic drag. The rockets could be fired in small groups or in a ripple salvo. It utilized the AN/APG-33 search radar coupled to an A-1B computing sight.

Again, the launcher was normally retracted into the bottom of the fuselage and was extended only during firing of the rockets much like the F-86D being developed at the same time. This arrangement was particularly advantageous because the clean aerodynamic lines of the aircraft were in no way altered as when rockets are carried externally. Even through a firing sequence, the drag created was only momentary, for the maximum period of extension was no more than 1.5 seconds – extension, retraction and firing cycles each required 0.5 seconds.

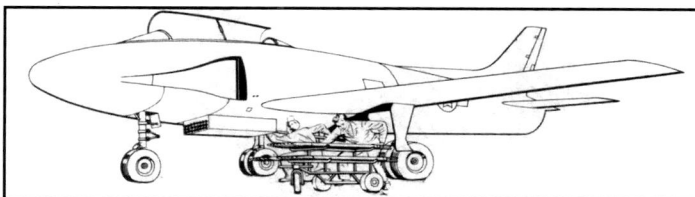

2-SEAT ALL-WEATHER INTERCEPTER

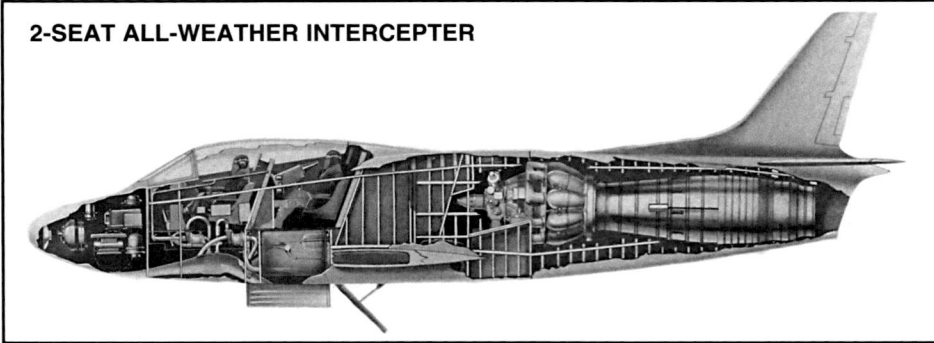

COCKPIT ACCESS

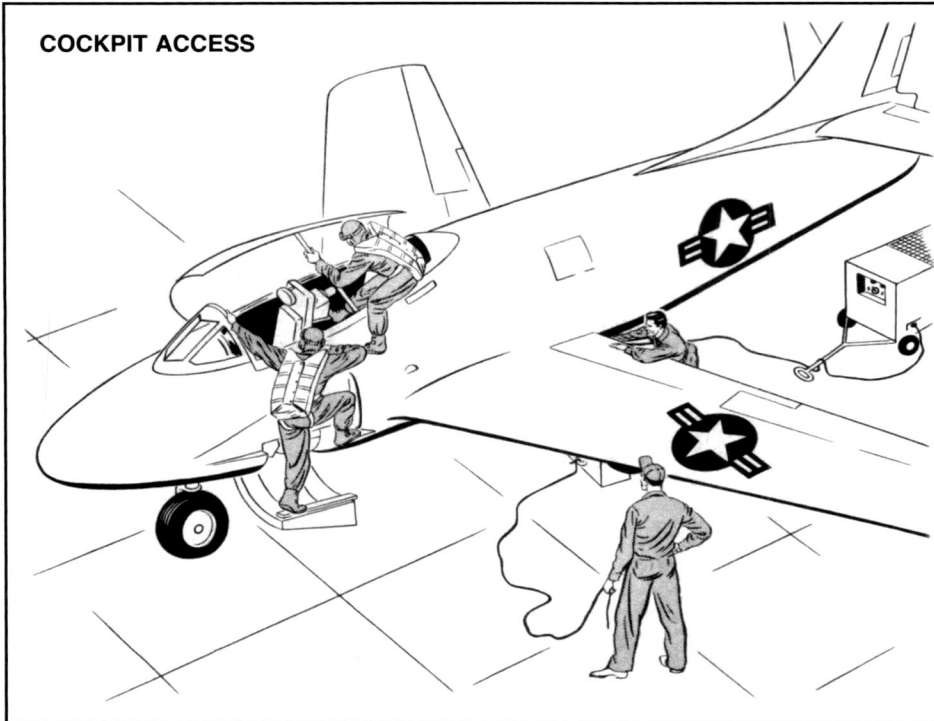

RADAR OPERATOR'S COCKPIT

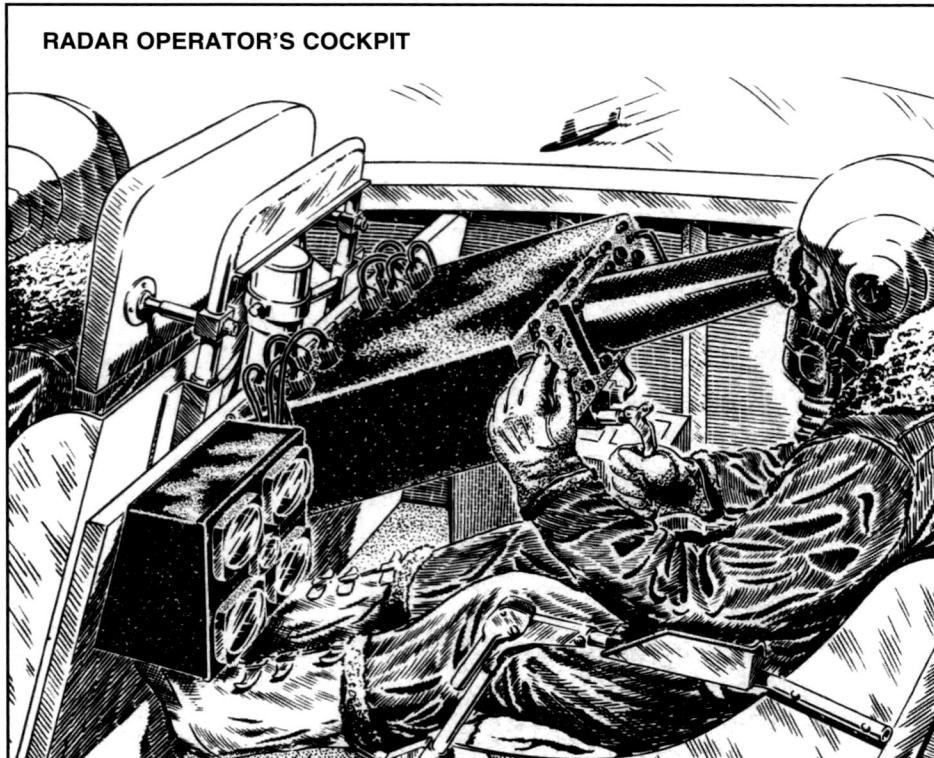

Through an intervalometer, small groups or the entire 24 rockets could be fired, the firing sequence being staggered between launch stations to avoid interference between the rocket fins.

Again, like the F-86D rocket pod system it incorporated a means of quick detachment which allowed the fastest time for loading of the rockets. Normally the rockets would be loaded singly from the rear, however with the quick detachment feature, the launcher could be loaded beforehand and switched out between each mission.

Electronic and Radar Equipment: The aircraft was to be equipped with the latest type electronic and radar equipment for its interceptor missions. Each piece of the system was to be strategically located and easily accessible to permit rapid ground servicing and replacement.

Electronic equipment included:
AN/APG-33 Radar
AN/APX-6 IFF
AN/APN-1 Radio Altimeter
AN/ARN-12 Marker Beacon
AN/ARC-3 VHF Command Radio
AN/ARN-6 Radio Compass
A-1B Gyro Computing Sight

Anti-Icing and De-Icing Systems: Like the single seat version, all weather operation of the aircraft was ensured by the use of heated wing and tail surfaces de-icing systems to be used in conjunction with a heated windshield anti-icing system. The surface de-icing system consisted of electrical heating pads applied to the internal surfaces of the wing and tail leading edges, deriving energy from a 40 kva alternator mounted directly on the engine power takeoff drive pad. To reduce the electrical power required to a minimum and provide adequate protection of the aircraft, power would have been cycled to various sections of the wing and tail surfaces. Windshield anti-icing would be accomplished by means of infrared lamps.

Additional Payload: Since this configuration had a gross weight of only 21,825 pounds as compared with the 26,516 pound design gross weight of the F-93A (at the time this study was conducted), alter loadings up to 4,700 pounds in external fuel, bombs or rockets were possible. These alternate loadings permitted an exceptional degree of versatility and adaptability for other tactical missions.

Performance: This design study resulted in an aircraft that could climb to 45,000 feet in 4.5 minutes or up to 40,000 in 3.4 minutes and had an endurance of two hours under both climb conditions. The aircraft retained the predicted outstanding performance of the F-93A. Excellent maneuverability, a maximum flight speed of 523 knots at 45,000 feet, and allowable dive speed of 1.05 Mach made possible rapid closure on the target aircraft were predicted. Furthermore, a wide range of level flight speeds were available between the maximum with afterburner and minimum with the speed brake extended.

Two-Place All-Weather Interceptor Design Study Performance Chart with a Pratt & Whitney J48-P-3

	Afterburning Plus Water-Alcohol		Afterburning	
	45,000 ft	Mil Thrust Combat Ceiling	45,000 ft	Mil Thrust Combat Ceiling
Takeoff Gross Weight, lb.	21,825	21,665	20,980	20,947
Fuel – Kerosene at 6.7 lb./gal, gal.	775	775	820	815
Water – Alcohol at 8.0 lb./gal, gal.	130	110	----------	----------
Combat Gross Weight, lb.	19,500	19,650	19,200	19,400
Combat Altitude, ft.	45,000	40,500	45,000	40,800
Time-to-Climb to Combat Altitude, min.	4.5	3.4	7.7	5.7
Afterburning Rate-of-Climb, ft/min.	1,350	2,780	1,450	2,750
Maximum Speed with Afterburning:				
Sea Level, kts.	616			
At Combat Altitude, kts.	523	532	524	532
Service Ceiling Afterburning Only, ft.	48,750	48,600	49,000	48,800
Military Trust Operating Altitude, ft.	41,400	40,500	41,800	40,800
Loiter Altitude, ft.	27,100	27,400	28,100	27,600
Time-to-Climb to 20,000 ft, min.	1.2	1.2	2.0	2.0
Time-to-Climb to 40,000 ft, min.	3.4	3.3	5.5	5.4
Endurance, hr.	2.0	2.0	2.0	2.0
Stall Speed, Flaps and Gear Down				
At Takeoff Gross Weight, kts.	118.0	117.5	116.0	116.0
At Landing Gross Weight, kts.	107.5	108.0	106.5	106.5
Landing Gross Weight and Fuel, lb/gal.	18,100/365	18,300/380	17,800/345	17,890/360
Takeoff Distance to Cleat 50 ft Obstacle, Flaps Down at Takeoff Gross weight with Afterburner Only, ft.	3,780	3,720	3,510	3,510
Landing Distance to Clear 50 Ft Obstacle at Landing Gross Weight, ft.	3,980	4,000	3,900	3,900

SINGLE PLACE INTERCEPTOR

A Single Place Interceptor design study was also conducted. The aircraft retained the basic aircraft configuration, but was modified to use single point refueling. It was to be powered by a J48-P-3 engine with an afterburner. Again, the heart of the avionics was the AN/APG-33 search and tracking radar modified for a single pilot operation. The armament was modified from the YF-93A six 20 mm guns to four 20 mm cannon with 200 rounds of ammunition per gun. An alternate to the cannon was a retractable launcher for twenty-four 2.75 inch rockets.

Single Place Interceptor Design Study Performance Chart

Takeoff Weight	19,623 lbs
Fuel	615 Gal
Takeoff Distance over 50 ft Obstacle	2,875 ft
Time-to-Climb to 45,000 ft	
Standing Start at Sea Level	6.25 min
Seal Level at Best Climb Speed	4.74 min
Endurance Standard Mission	1.3 hr
Performance Weight	17,833 lbs
Maximum Speed at 45,000 ft	538 kts
Service Ceiling	53,600 ft
Radius-of-Turn .85 Mach at an altitude of 45,000 ft	18,730 ft

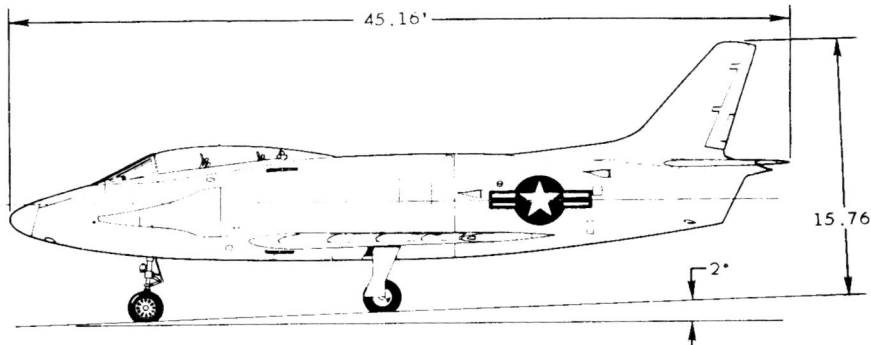

DIMENSIONAL DATA

WING
Sweepback	35°
Area	306.10 Sq Ft
Aspect Ratio	4.9
Taper Ratio	.502
Incidence (at root)	+1°
Incidence (at tip)	-1°

EMPENNAGE
Horizontal Tail
Area	46.09 Sq Ft
Span	14.83 Ft
Aspect Ratio	4.77
Taper Ratio	.451
Sweepback	35°
Stabilizer Deflection	
Up	3°
Down	9°

Vertical Tail
Area	33.46 Sq Ft
Span	7.32 Ft
Aspect Ratio	1.714
Taper Ratio	.368
Sweepback	35°

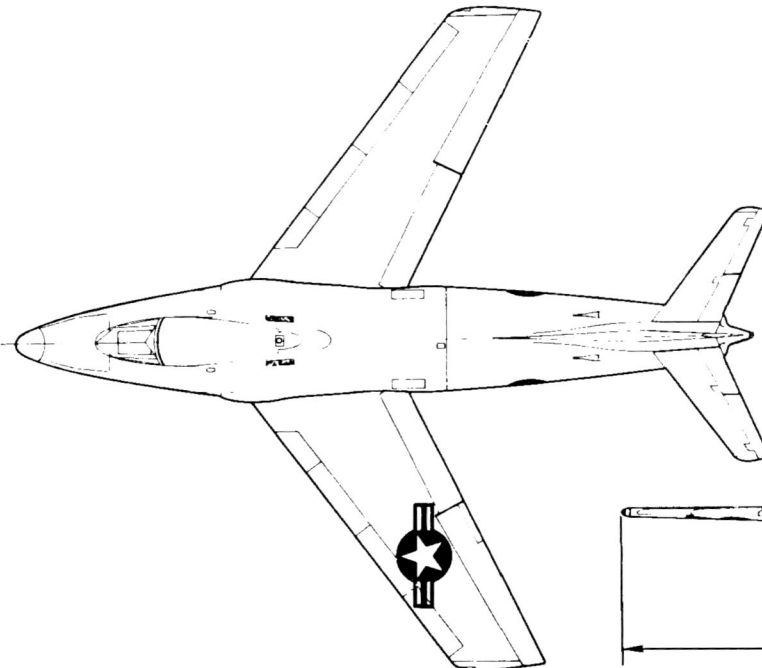

Two-Place All-Weather Interceptor Design Study

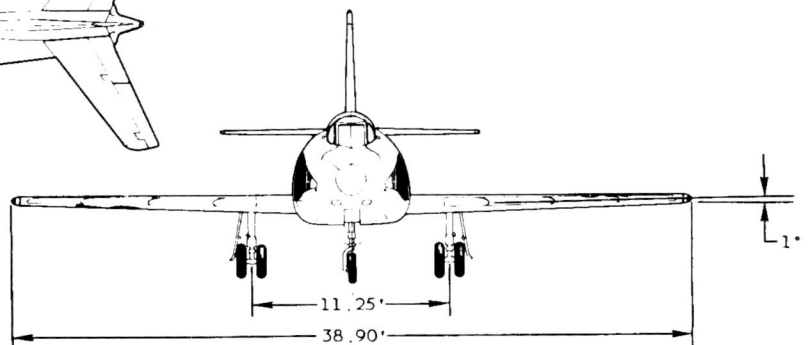

DAY RECONNAISSANCE

In addition to single place and two place fighters and interceptors, NAA proposed a day reconnaissance version of the F-93. As standard practice, all armament and its associated systems would be eliminated and replaced with cameras and their associated equipment. The armor protection for the pilot would be retained.

The RF-93 retained the wings, tails and landing gear of the F-93, but the nose forward of the pilot was to be extended approximately 47 inches and the radio equipment and battery would to be relocated forward to compensate for the weight of the armament equipment that was to be omitted. The pitot tube was to be relocated to a position above the forward optical window. The dual speed brakes on the bottom of the fuselage were replaced by a single unit.

Primary Vertical Camera Station: The primary vertical station was located in the fuselage nose section forward of the pilot. It could accommodate one of the following camera configurations:

1.) A Type K-17E, Day Reconnaissance Camera with three different lens cones of 6, 12 and 24-inch
2.) A Type K-22A Day Reconnaissance Camera with three different lens cones of 6, 12 and 24-inch.
3.) A Type T-9 Topographic Mapping Camera
4.) A Type S-7 Low Altitude High Speed Camera with 6 or 20-inch lens cones or an 88 mm lens cone
5.) A Type K-38 High Altitude Reconnaissance Camera with a 24-inch lens cone

The camera opening was to be covered by optically flat window glass which permitted 5 degree lateral tilt, a 6 degree forward tilt and a 2 degree aft tilt of the camera. Access to the primary vertical station for installation and servicing of the camera system and equipment would be through a removable access door located on the upper nose section.

Forward Oblique Camera Station: The forward oblique station was located in the forward portion of the nose section. Like the Primary Vertical Station, one of the following camera configurations could be accommodated:

1.) A Type K-22A Day Reconnaissance Camera with two different lens cones of 12 and 24-inch
2.) A Type A-10 35 mm Motion Picture Camera with 200 to 1,000 capacity film magazines
3.) A Type K-38 High Altitude Reconnaissance Camera with a 24-inch lens cone

The camera opening was to be covered by optically flat window glass. The camera could be depressed 12 degrees from the horizontal. Access to the forward oblique station for installation and servicing of the camera system and equipment would be through a removable access door located on the upper nose section.

Tri-Metrogon Camera Station: A tri-metrogon station was to be located in the forward fuselage below the cockpit. Metrogon is a high resolution, low-distortion, extra-wide field (90 degree field of view) photographic lens. A number of different camera configurations could be accommodated:

Three Type K-17C Charting Cameras with 6 inch lens cones and Type A-5A or Type A-9A film magazines.

The tri-metrogon cameras were to be mounted rigidly on a metal door structure that could be pivoted allowing complete access to the cameras and equipment for ground servicing and installation.

Side Oblique Camera Station: The following equipment was to be installed in the left oblique position just aft of the Tri-Metrogon Cameras:

1.) A Type K-22A Day Reconnaissance Camera with a 12-inch lens cone
2.) A Type S-7 Low Altitude, High Speed Camera with a 6 inch single, 7 inch stereo or an 88 mm lens cone

The camera opening would be covered by optically flat glass. A tilt adjustment of 6 degrees forward and 2 degrees aft was permitted.

Camera Doors: Somewhat unique to the RF-93 were flush doors remotely controlled from the cockpit to protect the photographic glass. All doors would operate simultaneously using electrically operated jack screws. The forward oblique window was not provided with a door as it was deemed that it was relatively free from possible taxi damage.

Cockpit Provisions: All of the cameras could be controlled from within the cockpit by the pilot. Three intervalometers were used to control the Forward Oblique Camera, the Primary Vertical Station and the Tri-Metrogon Camera Station.

An upright periscope viewfinder was to be installed in the cockpit above the instrument panel in place of the A-1B sight head. It was designed to be hinged to lie flat behind the panel when not in use. A streamlined fairing on the lower fuselage would protect the viewfinder objective lens.

Radio and Electronics: It was envisioned that radio equipment would be similar to that installed in the F-93A:

AN/ARC-3 Radio
SCR-695B Radio
AN/ARN-6 Radio Compass
AN/ARN-5A Radio Receiver
AN/ARN-12 Radio Receiver
RC-103 Marker Beacon

At left, 1 October 1948 artist illustration of the RF-93 reconnaissance proposal. (USAF)

Day Reconnaissance Design Study Performance Summary

Takeoff Gross Weight	25,726 lbs
Design Gross Weight	20,840 lbs
Maximum Speed at Sea Level:	
With Afterburner	615 kts
With Military Power	580 kts
With Normal Power	516 kts
Maximum Speed at 35,000 ft	
With Afterburner	540 kts
With Military Power	514 kts
Maximum Speed at 12,000 ft, at	
Normal Continuous Thrust	526 kts
Max Rate-of-Climb at Sea Level, Ft/Min	
Afterburner Thrust	12,000
With Military Thrust	5,640
With Normal Thrust	3,290

Time-to-Climb to 35,000 ft:	
With Afterburner Thrust	4.75 min
With Military Thrust	11.7 min
With Normal Thrust	22.9 min
Service Ceiling:	
With Afterburner Thrust	47,200 ft
With Military Thrust	41,200 ft
With Normal Thrust	37,200 ft
Combat Radius	706 nm
Average Speed	459 kts
Stall Speed, Power Off, Slats Extended, Flaps and Landing Gear Down:	
At Takeoff Gross Weight	128 kts
At Design Weight	115 kts
At Landing Weight	101 kts
Take-Off Over 50 ft Obstacle, No Wind, Flaps Down:	
With Afterburner at Gross Weight	5,100 Feet

Landing Distance to Clear A 50 Foot Obstaacle, No Wind, Zero Thrust:
At Landing Weight 3,600 ft

Notes:

Design gross weight over target equals take-off gross weight less 729 gallons of fuel (weight of aircraft before combat fuel is used).

Combat radius of action calculated in accordance with problem given for gas turbine powered fighter in tentative specification for standard aircraft characteristic charts.

Landing gross weight is takeoff weight less 90% fuel (16,192 pounds).

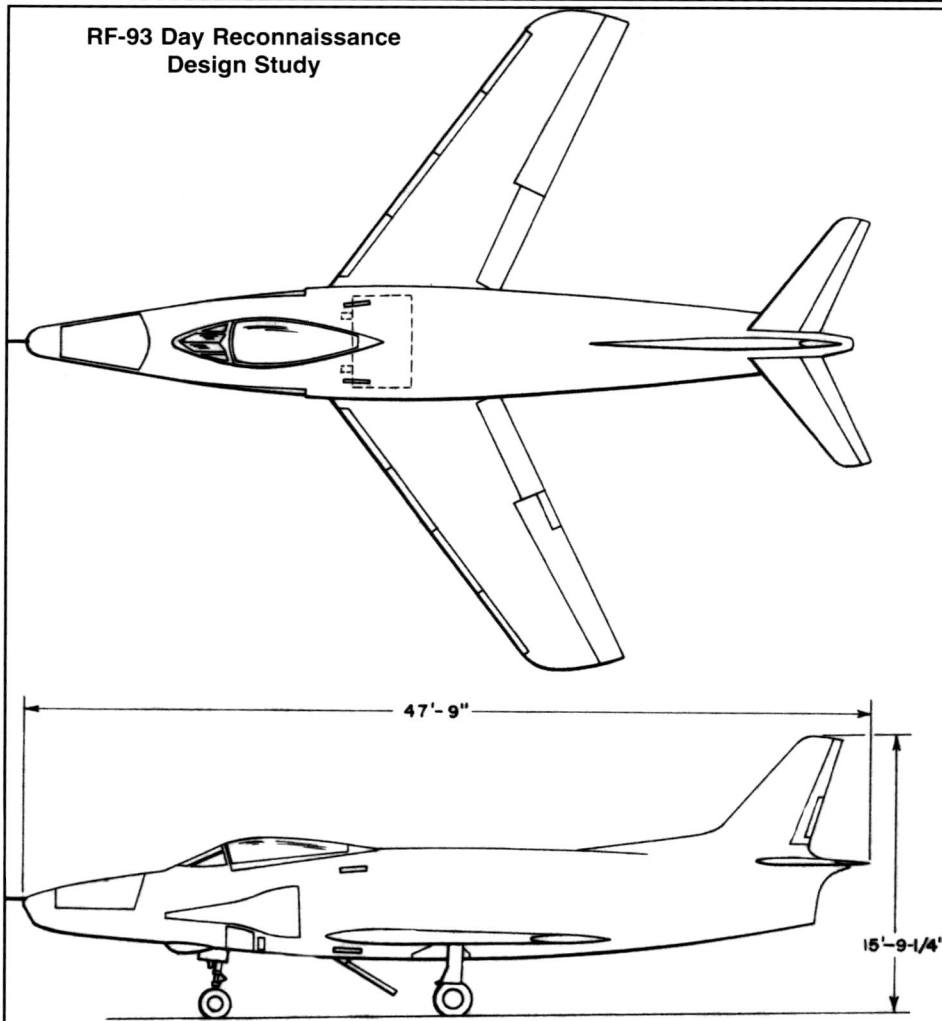

RF-93 Day Reconnaissance Design Study

47'-9"

15'-9-1/4"

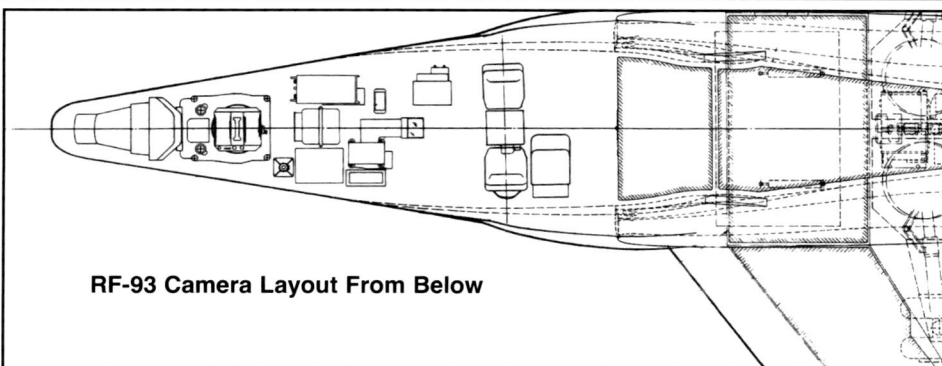

RF-93 Camera Layout From Below

FLIGHT TEST PROGRAMS

Air Force Flight Test Programs Phases: Flight test programs are normally broken into a number of phases, with each phase having a certain goal or milestone. At the time the YF-93A was in development, USAF required a standardized seven-phase flight test program for systematic evaluation of any new aircraft. New aircraft were tested by both the manufacturer and the Air Force. Most of the tests would be done at the Air Force Flight Test Center (AFFTC), Edwards AFB, CA.

Phase I was exclusively the manufacturer's flight test program, including first flight and early evaluation of handling qualities and performance, by company test pilots. Total flight time logged typically was 20 to 50 hours.

Phase II was the first USAF flight opportunity to verify that manufacturer's performance and aircraft's handling qualities figures were accurate and that the aircraft met its contract requirements. Total test hours varied from program to program.

Phase III was a second series of manufacturer's tests which evaluated changes or suggestions made by the USAF during Phase II testing. The time flown depended on the number and nature of those changes.

Phase IV was a second series of USAF tests, flown on the first aircraft built to production standards. Typically, 150 hours at AFFTC were flown in a detailed evaluation of performance, and stability and control. Flight data was used to develop performance charts for the Pilot's Handbook.

Phase V was the third series of USAF tests, and dedicated to all-weather testing.

Phase VI was accelerated service testing flown by USAF pilots at AFFTC with three

Above, George "Wheaties" Welch was North American's Chief Test Pilot for the YF-93 program. He flew all of the NAA Phase I test flights and all NAA follow-on tests. (NAA) Bottom, engine thrust calibration runs without the aft fuselage in place were conducted in December 1949 at North Base prior to the first flight of the YF-93. (NAA/Ginter collection)

or more early production aircraft. Pilots and maintenance personnel from user commands were invited to participate in this phase of flight test. Typical programs simulated routine operations – gunnery, bombing, night and bad weather flying -- were designed to prove overall suitability of new aircraft. Typical flight time logged was approximately 150 hours on each aircraft.

Phase VII was the USAF last round with a new aircraft. It was flown at the Air Proving Ground Command (APGC), Eglin AFB, FL, to assess the complete weapon system in conditions that simulated squadron service and combat environments.

The YF-93A flight test program only called for Phase I and II to be completed before a down select. The downfall of such an abbreviated flight test program meant that any defects found in the Air Force Phase II evaluation were not corrected. These would normally have been addressed by the manufacturer in Phase III and evaluated in Phase IV testing.

NAA PHASE I FLIGHT TEST RESULTS

The following data is taken directly from the 13 NAA Flight Test Reports held by the National Archives. These reports were still classified until the author requested them in September 2022. The reports are incomplete and contain numerous errors and conflicting data (missing flights and dates being the major ones).

The first YF-93A 48-317 was assigned to the Phase I effort while the second aircraft 48-318 was assigned to the Weapon Test Program. The NAA flight test monthly reports only cover test activity on 48-317, with 48-318 only being mentioned as a footnote. No NAA weapon related flight test reports have been located. As far as it can be determined, NAA never published a Flight Test results report. All reports located are incomplete.

Ground Thrust Calibration: Prior to the initial flight of the YF-93A airplane, ground thrust calibration tests were conducted. Tests made with the aft fuselage removed yielded thrust data in close agreement with the Pratt & Whitney acceptance test of the engine. Tests with the fuselage installed indicated that a thrust loss of 10.43 percent at 11,000 RPM was believed be attributed to the configuration of the afterburner shroud and aft fuselage cooling air ejector. This thrust loss was in substantial agreement with data obtained from the YF-93A engine test stand, on which a program to develop an optimum exhaust ejector and afterburner-shroud configuration was under way.

Engine test stand data indicated that little or no thrust loss was encountered when using an ejector fairing in which the exhaust nozzle to ejector throat distance was shorter than that of the airplane configuration. A new ejector with a length based on the test stand results was being developed to be installed on the airplane in order to increase the available net thrust.

Ground Structural Cooling Tests: Ground cooling tests conducted prior to the initial flight indicated that fuselage cooling was quite satisfactory. Temperatures in most areas were quite low, in fact some were slightly above ambient at 100% engine speed.

First Flight Pilot Comments: NAA Chief Test Pilot, George "Wheaties" Welch made the first flight of the YF-93A on 24 January 1950. The flight, which lasted 43 minutes, was conducted after a number of ground tests and both low and high speed taxi tests at North Base, Edwards AFB. He would go on to do all of the NAA test flights in the aircraft.

In his words: "The first flight on the YF-93A airplane was made on January 24 at Edwards Air Force Base. As delivery of the afterburner has been delayed, six JATO bottles were installed for assisted take-off. Three on the right side were fired during the take-off run at 145 knots (PIAS) [test boom indicated airspeed] using 20° flap. The airplane immediately became airborne. As the gear was being retracted and the flaps started up, the three left side JATO bottles were fired. The gear and flaps retracted with no noticeable sink."

"The airplane was climbed to 15,000 and rolls were done to the right and to the left at 320 knots (PIAS) to approximately 15 lbs. on the stick. Lateral control of the airplane was good and the stick forces were normal and similar to those obtained on an F-86A with the short chord ailerons. Elevator control was checked up to approximately 2.5 G. The force gradient was considered satisfactory."

"At 20,000 feet and 250 knots (PIAS) the speed brakes were extended. No trim change was noticeable, except that a slight push force (1.5 to 2 lbs.) was used at full extension. No trim change was noticed when the speed brakes were retracted. The speed brakes were also extended at 340 knots with only a small trim change again being noted. No buffet was felt either at 240 knots or 340 knots."

"A stall history was then made with gear and flaps down. A very slight air-

YF-93A NIGHT RUN-UP 10,700 R.P.M. - NO A/B. AFTERBURNER

plane buffet could be felt at 145 knots (PIAS). Slat operation was similar to slat operation in the F-86 with the new type slat although the slats opened 30 knots higher (approx. 170-180 knots (PIAS). As the elevator force required to decelerate the airplane was considerably higher than on the F-86, the stabilizer was used for trim. As the airplane decelerated, the general airplane buffet increased in intensity. At 125 knots the airplane rolled slightly, however, this was easily corrected with a slight aileron movement. The stall history was discontinued at this time. The rudder, aileron, and elevator were all very effective at 125 knots (PIAS), and, although a full stall was not attained (it was estimated that it would occur at about 110-115 knots PIAS)."

"The airplane was then returned to the field. Approach was made at 180 knots (PIAS). Sufficient flare and float were available to hold the airplane off the ground to approximately 125-130 knots. Touchdown occurred at 125 knots (PIAS) and was normal and similar to the F-86. The airplane rolled straight ahead during the landing, and brakes were used lightly to decelerate. The ground roll was considered satisfactory."

The NAA Phase I Flight Test program after first flight proceeded at a fairly rapid pace and for the most part was without major system problems. Testing did show that the aircraft had major issues with meeting its predicted performance parameters. Major event and issues discovered are summarized below.

Afterburner Operation: After a satisfactory operation of the afterburner on the ground, afterburner ignitions tests were made in flight at 15,000 feet during Flights 3 and 4. Ignition occurred in 4 to 5 seconds after actuation of the afterburner switch and the nozzle eyelids operated satisfactorily. Ignition was maintained for 30 seconds on Flight 3 and for 2 minutes on Flight 4. During both runs, tailpipe temperature exceeded the limit upon ignition and it was necessary to reduce engine speed to about 10,900 RPM in order to maintain the limiting temperature of 720°C.

Stability and Control: Preliminary data was obtained on flight 15 at a forward C.G. The static lateral directional and longitudinal stability was found to be very similar to that obtained on the F-86A. Accelerated longitudinal stability data also obtained indicated a lightening of stick-free stability near the maximum test G.

Accelerated longitudinal stability

tests were conducted on the number 1 aircraft (Flight 18) along with a similar test on the number 2 aircraft (Flight 1). Both aircraft agreed quite closely and no force reversals were noted.

A static longitudinal stability test was made on the number one YF-93A (Flight 18) along with a similar test on the number two aircraft (Flight 1). Results were in good agreement since positive stability was demonstrated up to approximately 400 knots VE and became neutrally stable at speeds above this.

Static Lateral Directional Stability (Sideslip) tests accomplished on the number 2 aircraft during its first flight showed that the static lateral directional stability characteristics agreed closely with those of the number 1 aircraft except for the aileron stick force gradients. NAA attributed this to a variation in aileron boost valve operation.

After the Air Force Phase II Testing was complete, NAA continued to test and tune the aircraft's stability and control.

Trim Change due to Speed Brake Opening: The effect of opening the speed brakes on longitudinal trim was

Above, YF-93 take-off characteristics were normal with the exception of a rather long roll and flat angle of initial climb. Take-offs were made with both 20° flaps and full flaps (approximately 38°). However, the full flap configuration proved more satisfactory and resulted in a noticeably shorter take-off roll. (USAF) Bottom, the early 1950s were a very busy time for NAA with a multitude of projects. NAA's North Base facility shows a RB-45C in the background with the YF-93A in the foreground with the YF-95A (later renamed YF-86D). (Ginter collection)

checked during Flight 18 of the first YF-93A. A fairly large elevator angle change occurred when the speed brakes were opened, especially at high speeds. The elevator hinge moments and stick forces for these elevator angle changes were noted to be very moderate.

Pilot George Welch commented that at 400 knots or above, a slight snaking of the aircraft occurred when the speed brakes were opened and the afterburner was on. The snaking seemed to increase with a corresponding increase in speed. However, as determined by a later check, no snaking occurred at these speeds when either the afterburner or speed

Above, failure of the ram air duct following flight 10 on 13 March 1950. (NAA)

Above, failure of the lower right bleed air duct following flight 10 on 13 March 1950. (NAA) Below, NAA employee has his hand in the upper right bleed air duct (found on NACA intakes) of ship one at LAX. Note original tail-cone profile. (Ginter collection)

bakes were not operated. Since the condition of afterburner on and speed brakes open is not considered normal practice, the snaking condition was not thought to be critical.

Canopy Opening Checks: A canopy opening check was made during Flight 10. Checks were made at approximately 210, 225, 235 and 260 KIAS at 11,000 ft. The canopy opening at 210 and 225 KIAS was accomplished in 3 to 4 seconds. At 235 and 260 KIAS, the maximum canopy opening obtained was six inches.

BOUNDARY LAYER DUCT AND MAIN ENGINE DUCT SKIN FAILURES: Inspection of the airplane following Flight 10 of the first YF-93A revealed skin failures in the following areas:

1. Cracking of the inner face skin in the lower bleed duct on the right hand side.
2. Buckle in the outer face of the main duct wall forward of the front spar on the left hand side.
3. Canning of the inner wall of the main duct on the left hand side.
4. Five inch crack along a row of rivets on the inner wall of the bleed at the entrance on the right hand side.
5. Failure of the emergency ram air duct.

PERFORMANCE

By the end of March 1950, NAA realized that the YF-93A was not performing as designed. In comparison with estimated data the high speed test results obtained at 15,000 feet showed a loss in speed of approximately 25 knots for augmented power and 94 knots for military power. Actual climbs were also low. NAA was convinced that the reasons for the loss in performance of the airplane in comparison with the estimates were:

1. Jet interference, which appears mostly in flight and increases in magnitude with flight speed.
2. Pratt & Whitney estimated engine thrust data were higher than obtained with the flight test engine. The engine manufactur-

er's engine data used in the performance estimates showed a military power static rating of 6,250 lbs. The actual military power static rating was 6,000 lbs.

3. Low tailpipe temperatures.

The above reasons for losses in performance were substantiated on the YF-95A airplane (later the designation was changed from YF-95A to YF-86D). Tests of the YF-95A showed a marked increase in performance when a straight tailpipe installation, exiting close to the rear or aft of the fuselage, was used in place of the standard afterburner tailpipe and shroud.

To further evaluate the above loss in performance, survey rakes were installed in the tailpipe nozzle and aft of the nozzle (across the fuselage exit area) to evaluate the thrust interference characteristics in flight. Various modifications to the fuselage aft end and tailpipe location were started in design and construction for availability at the end of the rake investigation. A wind tunnel program using a small jet engine was also used.

Analysis of data obtained during Flights 11 and 12 with the survey rake installed indicated the thrust of the engine to be up to specification and no losses were incurred due to jet interference.

An investigation was then conducted to establish the cause of the speed losses. The major cause of the speed loss was considered to be an increment of drag caused by a disturbed airflow over the fuselage. In order to determine the disturbed areas, the entire right side of the fuselage of the airplane and portion of the wing and stabilizer were tufted prior to Flight 13. Photographs of the tufted airplane were obtained at airspeeds of 220, 240, 260, 290, 330 and 445 KIAS. Examination of the tuft pictures revealed disturbances along the outer edges of the inlet duct and aft of the boundary layer bleed duct existed.

After the tuft survey of Flight 13 wind tunnel tests were conducted to determine the optimum inlet duct configuration. Results of these tests indicated that straight ramp fairings with rounded edges leading into the duct entrance had less drag than the original ramp fairing. It was also determined that a half cone hood over the boundary layer bleed duct exit gave a further reduction in drag.

On Flights 16 and 17, conducted on 17 May 1950, performance data runs at 15,000 feet with the modified flush inlets showed an increase in high speed at military power of 25 knots with the bleed

hoods on and 20 knots with the bleed hoods off, in comparison with data obtained with the original inlet duct configuration. Augmented power results showed no apparent change in speeds with the modified inlet ducts, bled hoods on or off.

At this time the first aircraft (48-317) was turned over to the Air Force for Phase II Testing. NAA only had the opportunity to test the modified flush inlets on three flights, about 3 hours of flight time, insufficient time to evaluate the modification over the entire flight envelope.

At top, NAA used a survey rake to determine the installed J48 engine performance. The rake measured the pressure and temperature of the exhaust. (NAA/Boeing via Mike Lombardi) Above, ship one was fitted with an exhaust survey rake for flights 11 and 12. (Ginter collection) Below, on flight 13 photographs of the tufted airplane were obtained at airspeeds of 220, 240, 260, 330, and 445 kIAS. Examination revealed disturbances along the outer edges of the inlet duct and aft of the boundrey layer bleed duct existed. (Boeing) Bottom, low speed wind tunnel tests indicated the drag of the YF-93 could be reduced by refairing the inlet ducts and installing hoods over the duct boundry layer bleed outlets. (NAA)

Air Force Phase II Flight Test Program:

The flight test program was conducted to obtain quantitative data pertaining to the performance and stability and control characteristics of the airplane, and to qualify Air Force pilots in the airplanes prior to an Air Force evaluation. All flights were conducted using the first YF-93A 48-317 with its refaired flush inlet ducts and the original aft fuselage. A total of 17 flights, utilizing 13 hours and 43 minutes of flying time, were made between 23 May and 5 June 1950 for the purpose of obtaining quantitative data. During the same period, 8 flights were made for the purpose of pilot qualification. All flights were made from Edwards Air Force Base, Muroc, California.

Air Force Phase II Flight Test Results:
The following are excerpts of the never published Air Force YF-93A Phase II Test Report written by then Major Frank Kendall "Pete" Everest Jr. Starting in February 1946 he was assigned to the Flight Test Division at Wright-Patterson Air Force Base in Ohio as a test pilot. While assigned to the Flight Test Division, he was temporary assigned to Edwards AFB as the lead Air Force test pilot on the YF-93A. Author's comments are enclosed in [.....].

PHASE II FLIGHT TEST OF THE YF-93A AIRPLANE, USAF NO. 48.317

Purpose: "The purpose of this report is to present the results of the Phase II flight tests of the North American YF-93A airplane, USAF No 48-317."

Description of the Airplane: "The YF-93A was a single-place, low-wing, penetration fighter with sweptback wings and empennage. Characteristic features of the airplane include a controllable horizontal stabilizer, leading edge slats, flush engine air-intakes ducts, dual speed brakes which are mounted side-by-side and extend from the under-side of the fuselage. The landing gear is tricycle type with the nose gear retracting forward into the nose section of the fuselage and the main gear retracting inward into the inner wing panels and fuselage. The main gear consists of dual wheels mounted side-by-side. The airplane is powered by a J48-P-2 (Pratt and Whitney JT-7A) turbojet engine with afterburner. [This is in error. The J48-P-2 engine used water injection instead of an afterburner. The YF-93A had no provision to carry water.] The afterburner incorporates a two position nozzle which is circular in both the open and closed positions. Single-slotted trailing edge flaps extend spanwise from the ailerons to the fuselage and slats are incorporated in the leading edge of the wing."

Weight and Balance: "The airplane was weighted by the contractor with an electric weighting kit and the operation was witnessed by Air Force personnel. The gross weight at which the airplane was weighted and at which the majority of the test flights were flown was 24,400 pounds. This loading included 995 gallons of ANF-48 fuel (100-130 octane) at 6 pounds per gallon, 2,550 pounds of ballast to replace the armament and give a desirable CG loca-

tion, 2.3 gallons of oil, and a crew weight of 190 pounds. The CG location at this gross weight was 18.8% MAC with the landing gear extended or 18.6% MAC with the landing gear retracted. The full internal fuel of the airplane was 1,555 gallons. However, flights at this gross weight required the use of JATO for take-off and consequently only one flight was made with this loading. The take-off gross weight for the full fuel condition was 29,980 pounds which included 6 JATO units mounted on the underside of the fuselage."

Cockpit Description: "Access to the cockpit is gained either by means of a ladder or use of steps provided in the side of the fuselage. Either method, however, requires assistance from the ground. Entry to the cockpit might be gained without aid, but would require climbing over the canopy and would not be generally practical."

"In general layout of the cockpit was very satisfactory. Although the ejection seat is adjustable only vertically, sufficient adjustment is available. Also, the rudder pedals are adjustable, fore and aft, and are interconnected to assure even alignment after adjustment. With the exception of the bomb and rocket switches, which were inaccessible when the seat was adjusted full up, all controls were easily reached. The throttle travel was considered too great in forward movement. Also, this extreme forward position blanked out the oxygen pressure gage. The control stick was a "double-pivot" type and was satisfactory except the grip. The grip used was considered too large and bulky for comfort."

"Visibility from the cockpit was unsatisfactory. The cockpit was too large to permit unrestricted side or rearward visibility and forward vision was limited by the high instrument panel. The split bulletproof windshield was undesirable because of distortion which it caused. In order to land it was necessary to look out either the right or left windshield to judge height correctly."

"The cockpit lighting was excellent with the exception of the landing gear

At top left, Major Frank "Pete" Kendall Everest was in command of the Air Force Phase II testing and flew nearly 100% of the flights. (USAF) At left, the small, but very dedicated NAA flight test team in front of the first YF-93A at North Base, Edwards AFB, CA. (NAA)

warning light which was far too bright and with no provision for dimming. There was a minimum of reflection and glare from the canopy and side windshields. However, the forward bullet-proof windshield was most objectionable because of undue reflection of ground lights and previously mentioned distortion, when landing."

Taxing and Ground Handling: "The nose wheel steering was particularly noteworthy. Response was quick and definite and the feeling of complete control and maneuverability was present at all times. This proved true in moderate cross winds encountered and upon all surfaces used for taxing or takeoff. Vision while taxing was fair, although downward vision was restricted at all times as previously mentioned. Braking was exceptionally good, with positive action and ease of operation. Because of the relatively heavy weight of the airplane an unusually large amount of power was necessary for taxing. For this reason, it was necessary to exercise extreme care of the direction of the jet blast when taxiing."

Takeoff and Initial Climb: "The take-off characteristics and technique required were normal with the exception of a rather long roll and flat angle of the initial climb. Initial directional control was maintained by use of the nose wheel steering until an indicated speed of approximately 87 knots (100 mph) was attained, at which time the rudder became sufficiently effective. For the take-off the rudder and aileron trim tabs were set at neutral and the horizontal stabilizer was set for 5° of nose-up trim. Take-offs were made with both 20° flaps and full flaps (approximately 38°). However, the full flap configuration proved more satisfactory and resulted in a noticeably shorter take-off roll. As a result, on take-offs made from the dry lake bed it was estimated that approximately 1500 ft would be added to the take-off roll, were the speed brakes inadvertently left in the down position. Several take-offs were made from the concrete runway and were measured by use of a photo grid. The data obtained from these measurements have been corrected to standard sea level, no wind condition and are summarized in the following table":

"One take-off was measured at a gross weight of 27,800 pounds utilizing six JATO units. This take-off, corrected to standard sea level, no wind conditions, resulted in a ground roll of 5,910 feet and a total distance over a 50 foot obstacle of 7,000 feet. The indicated airspeed for this take-off was 144 knots (166 mph) at take-off and 157 knots (181 mph) at 50 feet. Corresponding true speeds, corrected as before to sea level, were 170 knots (196 mph) at take-off and 175 knots (202 mph) at 50 feet. The JATO units were fired in groups of three. The first set was fired at an indicated airspeed of 124 knots (143 mph) and the second set approximately 10-12 seconds later. It did appear, however, that for optimum performance over a 50 foot obstacle it might have been advantageous to fire the first set at a speed a few knots slower that actually used."

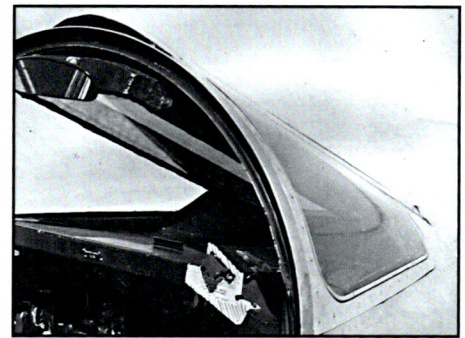

Above, the YF-93A had a three-piece windshield (see page 18). The side panels were curved like the early F-86As. The center section was made in two parts. The outer windshield was made of two panels forming a V, while the inner panel was made of a thick armor glass. In this view the thickness of the flat inside face of armor glass is very apparent. It was a source of problems because of reflection of ground lights and distortion when landing. (NARA)

AIR FORCE PHASE II FLIGHT LOG YF-93A 48-317					
AF Flight No.	Date	Pilot	Duration	Phase II Data Flight	Test/Remarks
1	23 May 50	Everest	00:41	No	Pilot Checkout
2	23 May 50	Everest	00:43	No	Airspeed Calibration
3	23 May 50	Johnson	00:47	Yes	Pilot Check Out, Stalls
4	23 May 50	Boyd	00:35	No	Pilot Checkout
5	23 May 50	Murray	00:44	Yes	Stick Force/g
6	26 May 50	Newman	00:40	No	Pilot Checkout
7	26 May 50	Everest	00:51	Yes	Quick Climbs, Speed Power at 10,000 Feet
8	27 May 50	Everest	01:11	Yes	Quick Climbs, Speed Power at 20,000 Feet
9	27 May 50	Everest	00:44	Yes	Quick Climbs, Max Speed Points
10	27 May 50	Everest	01:14	Yes	Quick Climb, Speed Power at 30,000 Feet
11	28 May 50	Everest	01:05	Yes	Quick Climbs, Speed Power at 10,000 Feet
12	28 May 50	Johnson	00:15	No	Flight Abort
13	29 May 50	Everest	01:10	Yes	Stability and Control
14	30 May 50	Everest	00:23	Yes	Ferry to South Base Max Speed at 5,000 ft
15	30 May 50	Everest	00:05	Yes	Measured Takeoff/Landing - Right Main Inboard Tire Blew on Landing.
16	30 May 50	Everest	00:45	Yes	Measured Takeoff/Landing
17	30 May 50	Everest	00:10	No	Ferry Flight to back to North Base
18	31 May 50	Everest	00:48	Yes	Stability and Control
19	1 June 50	Everest	00:50	Yes	Rate of Roll
20	1 June 50	Everest	01:00	Yes	Night Flight
21	2 June 50	Everest	00:50	Yes	Rate of Roll, Maneuvering Stability
22	2 June 50	Newman	00:34	No	Pilot Checkout
23	2 June 50	Murray	00:32	No	Pilot Checkout
24	2 June 50	Ascani	00:48	No	Pilot Checkout
25	5 June 50	Everest	01:08	Yes	Heavy Weight Takeoff – Aft fuselage explosion occurred due to a leak in the afterburner fuel drain line during an attempted take-off. Major damage. Last AF Phase II flight.

Take-off No.	Gross Weight Lbs.	Total Distance Required to Clear 50-ft Obstacle, ft.	Speeds 50-ft. IAS Knots (mph)	Speeds 50-ft. V₁ Knots (mph).	Ground Roll Distance ft.	Speed at Break-Away IAS Knots (mph)	Speed at Break-Away V₁ Knots (mph)
1	24,600	6,220	156 (180)	166 (191	4,600	145 (167)	150 (172)
2	23,700	5,210	150 (173)	160 (184)	3,830	141 (162)	145 (167)
3	22,400	5,050	155 (178)	153 (176)	3,600	143 (165)	136 (157)
4	21,100	4,960	148 (170)	168 (193)	3,690	142 (163)	157 (181)
5	19,800	4,480	151 (174)	169 (194)	3,575	142 (163)	151 (174)

"After take-off the landing gear and flaps could be retracted immediately with no appreciable trim change or loss of altitude. However, it was necessary to exercise care during take-off roll, so as not to allow the nose of the airplane to rise to such an angle as would result in the inducement of excessive drag and thereby appreciably extend the take-off distance."

Climb Performance: "Climbs were flown both with the afterburner off and with the afterburner on and also at two gross weights at engine start, 24,400 pounds and 28,300 pounds. The climb for the 24,400 pound gross weight and with afterburner on were flown at several different speed schedules. "

"Because of a temporary restriction, at the time the tests were flown, the afterburner was limited to five minutes of continuous operation. This necessitated flying the climbs in segments of approximately five minutes duration, although the data has been corrected to correspond to continuous climbs."

Stall Characteristics: "Stalls were performed with the airplane clean and in the take-off and landing configurations and accelerated stalls were performed in the clean configuration. In all of the unaccelerated stalls the airplane stalled straight ahead in a mild manner and the recovery was accomplished easily. The warning consisted of an airframe buffet and occurred at approximately 15 miles per hour before the stall in all cases except in the landing configuration where no warning was detected. In the accelerated stalls, which were performed in "wind-up" turns, the airplane would buffet and "mush" if held in the stall and would recover if the back pressure on the stick was released. Failure of either leading edge slat to extend during the accelerated stalls, would cause a premature stalling of one wing and would result in a definite rolling action. At higher altitudes (20,000 to 30,000 feet) and at the heavier gross weights the airplane would fall or "mush" with no apparent stall warning and no buffeting to indicate a stall. This was demonstrated with full up elevator. Some of the stalls which were performed are summarized in the table at right:"

Stability and Control: "In order to reduce the control forces in flight, an open center hydraulic system supplying boost pressure for movement of the ailerons and elevators was incorporated in the airplane. Hydraulic pressure was supplied to this system by means of an engine-driven hydraulic pump. Should this system have

CLIMB PERFORMANCE

For a gross weight at engine start of 24,400 pounds and with the afterburner on:

Altitude Feet	Rate-of-Climb Feet/Min	Time-to-Climb Minutes	Fuel Used Pounds	Distance NM	True Speed Knots
Sea Level	6,450	—	—	—	350
5,000	5,800	0.80	200	4	360
10,000	5,200	1.70	400	10	360
15,000	4,550	2.80	620	16	355
20,000	3,900	4.00	850	23	350
25,000	3,300	5.30	1,075	31	345
30,000	2,650	7.10	1,330	40	340

For a gross weight at engine start of 28,300 pounds and with the afterburner on:

Altitude Feet	Rate-of-Climb Feet/Min	Time-to-Climb Minutes	Fuel Used Pounds	Distance NM	True Speed Knots
Sea Level	5,200	—	—	—	335
5,000	4,650	1.00	250	6	330
10,000	4,050	2.20	500	12	330
15,000	3,500	3.50	750	19	330
20,000	2,900	5.00	1,000	27	325
25,000	2,400	6.90	1,275	38	325
30,000	1,800	9.30	1,600	52	320

For a gross weight at engine start of 24,600 pounds and with the afterburner inoperative:

Altitude Feet	Rate-of-Climb Feet/Min	Time-to-Climb Minutes	Fuel Used Pounds	Distance NM	True Speed Knots
Sea Level	3,050	—	—	—	270
5,000	2,650	1.80	190	8	278
10,000	2,250	3.80	390	17	282
15,000	1,850	6.20	600	28	282
20,000	1,450	9.30	840	43	280

LEVEL FLIGHT PERFORMANCE

"Maximum flight level performance was determined at approximately every 5,000 feet from 5,000 to 30,000 feet, with full engine and afterburner and maximum engine power only."

Maximum Speed:

Altitude Feet	Afterburner On Knots (mph)	Afterburner Off Knots (mph)	Recommended Cruse Speed VT	Nautical Air Mile Per Pound of Fuel
Sea Level	574 (661)	470 (561)	—	—
5,000	575 (662)	472 (546)	—	—
10,000	575 (662)	471 (543)	398 (458)	0.820
15,000	573 (660)	467 (538)	—	—
20,000	568 (654)	459 (529)	390 (449)	0.110
25,000	555 (639)	451 (520)	—	—
30,000	538 (630)	440 (507)	381 (439)	0.134

STALL CHARACTERISTICS

"The accelerated stalls Nos. 4 and 5 were accomplished at an altitude of approximately 18,000 feet, and stall No. 9 was accomplished at approximately 25,000 feet."

Stall No.	Flap Position	Gear Position	Speed Brakes	Approx. Accel. "g"	Warning IAS Knots(mph)	Stall IAS Knots(mph)	Gross Weight lb.
1	Up	Up	In	1.0	165 (190)	145 (167)	22,000
2	Up	Up	Out	1.0	165 (190)	152 (175)	21,850
3	20°	Down	In	1.0	148 (170)	137 (158)	21,700
4	Up	Up	In	2.0	215 (247)	210 (292)	21,550
5	Up	Up	In	3.0	282 (325)	278 (320)	21,400
6	Full	Down	Out	1.0	135 (155)	135 (155)	21,250
7	Full	Down	Out	2.0	165 (190)	165 (190)	21,050
8	20°	Down	In	1.7	158 (182)	158 (182)	20,900
9	Up	Up	In	2.9	243 (280)	239 (275)	19,500

failed or had engine failure occurred, the control forces would have been considerably increased but the airplane would remain controllable. There was no noticeable friction in the aileron or rudder systems, however, this was not true of the elevator, i.e., the stick could be displaced fore or aft and friction forces were so high as to prevent its return to a neutral position. After several flights were made under these circumstances, a bungee was installed to alleviate this condition and proved to be a considerable aid."

Longitudinal Stability: "Dynamic longitudinal stability appeared satisfactory throughout the speed range flown. Oscillations imposed by introducing abrupt positive or negative accelerations, were damped quickly and positively."

"The accelerated stability of the airplane was evaluated by performing a "sick force per g" test at different airspeeds in the cruise configuration. These tests were performed both with and without the bungee installed. The maneuvering stability without the bungee installed was unsatisfactory. The pound of force per g gradient is very small and shows a definite flattening. The forces required for an acceleration were less than the control friction forces and the control stick would not return to neutral from a displaced position. With the bungee installed, forces were normal with the exception of speeds near the stall at which there was a force reversal. This condition is not critical, however, as the airplane would stall before the limit load factor could be obtained."

[Control or force reversal is an adverse effect on the controllability of aircraft. The flight controls reverse themselves in a way that is not intuitive, so pilots may not be aware of the situation and therefore provide the wrong inputs, A common example can be found in roll stability. The problem occurs when the amount of airflow over the wing becomes so great that the force generated by the ailerons is enough to twist the wing itself, due to insufficient torsional stiffness of the wing structure. For instance, when the aileron is deflected upwards in order to make that wing move down, the wing twists in the opposite direction. The net result is that the airflow is directed down instead of up and the wing moves upward, opposite of what was expected. In longitudinal stability, pitch, the flow on the elevator is changed because of fuselage bending and flow interference caused by the fuselage.]

"There were no undesirable trim change characteristics. With extension of the landing gear, lowering of the flaps, or changes in power, the trim changes were very small and could easily be controlled by normal stick forces. However, with the extension of the speed brakes at high speed a definite "pitch-up" would occur, although this was not as pronounced or severe as experienced with other present day production fighter type aircraft. This characteristic was not considered critical unless the speed brakes were opened while operating the aircraft near the critical load factor."

Directional Stability: "Dynamic directional stability appeared to be within the specification requirements. Major oscillations incited by abrupt rudder deflections appeared to dampen out entirely in 3 1/2 – 4 cycles and no small amplitude oscillations seemed to persist."

"Rudder forces were normal and increased considerably with an increase in speed. However, at an indicated Mach number of 0.89 a steady, small amplitude, movement of the rudder appeared which could not be stopped by applying force to the rudder pedals. This condition was transient, however, and did not appear at higher or lower Mach numbers. There were no directional trim changes evident at any time."

Lateral Stability: "Rate of roll were performed at several different speeds at 10,000 and 25,000 feet. Lateral dynamic stability was satisfactory. There were no noticeable oscillations. The stick, however, had a poor centering device and in stick free stability would not return entirely to neutral. Aileron forces were normal, however, the aileron breakout forces [The minimum pilot control force necessary to make the airplane pitch, roll, or yaw is called the breakout force.] were high and at first impression gave indication of high aileron forces. There were no noticeable trim changes with the exception that at .92 indicated Mach number a left and then a right wing heaviness was encountered.

This is easily corrected with stick and is not considered critical. There was a slight aileron buffet when the flaps were down, however, this also was not considered critical."

Dives: "Because of the limited available afterburner operation and the inability of the airplane to reach acceptable altitudes under atmospheric conditions encountered, no high Mach number dives were attempted. One dive was attempted, however, from an altitude of approximately 30,000 feet and an indicated Mach number of 0.92 was attained. The afterburner was utilized for this dive. The dive was entered by half-rolling the airplane until a dive angle of approximately 45 to 50 degrees was obtained. The airplane was then rolled out and held until an altitude of 18 to 20,000 feet was reached and the speed began to decrease. Recovery was accomplished by relaxing forward pressure on the stick and was normal in every way. During the dive no unusual trim changes or control forces were encountered, although at an indicated Mach of 0.92 there was a slight rudder buffet or "nibble" which ceased immediately with an increase in speed. At an indicated Mach number of 0.92, the left wing dropped sharply and was followed by an identical dropping of the right wing. These trim changes were easily controllable by the stick and were not considered critical. There was a natural increase of push force on the stick to maintain the dive, although this force could easily be trimmed out by adjustment of the horizontal stabilizer."

Approach and Landing: "A normal tactical traffic pattern [Also called an overhead traffic pattern. The overhead pattern is an energy depleting maneuver used to slow the aircraft in the landing pattern - a sharp, 180-degree turn (the break or peel

---

The Air Force Phase II testing ended on 5 June 1950 when 48-317 experienced an explosion in the aft fuselage. Above, right side of the aft fuselage blown open. (NARA) Botom, left side of the rear fuselage showing the line of severed rivets and a large dent. (NARA)

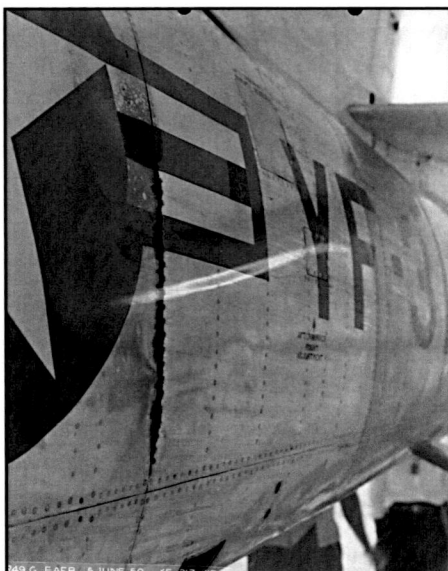

off) to the downwind, configure for landing, and then another 180-degree turn to final approach.] was used without difficulty although the airspeeds maintained were necessarily higher than usual because of the relatively high wing loading of the airplane. [wing loading is the total mass of an aircraft divided by the area of its wing] Although the landing gear could be extended at any time after the "peel off" during the tactical pattern, it was advisable to retract the speed brakes immediately. This was done as a precautionary measure taken because level flight could not be maintained with the gear extended, the flaps down, and the speed breaks out, without the use of the afterburner. Flaps were extended and maximum engine power was applied in case of a "go-around". An indicated airspeed of approximately 173 knots (200 mph) was maintained on the base leg and final approach with an "over the fence" at

a speed of 150 knots (173 mph) and touch down was accomplished at approximately 139 knots (160 mph). Immediately upon touchdown the speed brakes were extended to aid in deceleration during the landing roll. Care must be exercised during the touchdown and subsequent roll to avoid dragging the tail of the airplane on the runway. The rudder was sufficiently effective to maintain directional control down to indicated air speeds of approximately 61 knots (70 mph) at which time it was permissible to utilize nose wheel steering. In the case of a wave-off or "go-around", full power was applied, the landing gear, flaps, and speed brakes were retracted and the afterburner ignited as soon as possible. However, the success of a "go-around" would be questionable at an indicated air speed of less than 174 knots (200 mph)."

"The same pattern and procedures were used for night landings. The landing lights were satisfactory although the taxi lights proved of little value because of their low intensity. The landing lights could be utilized as taxi lights but were unsatisfactory for this purpose as the most desirable angle of the settings for landings proved too low for use while taxiing."

"Several landings were measured by use of a photo theodolite and the data obtained has been corrected to standard sea level, no wind conditions and is summarized in the following table below:"

General Aircraft and System Functioning: "The afterburner controls installed were satisfactory. However, it would be desirable to have faster operation of the amplifier control in regards to regulation of the tailpipe temperature. There was a lag of 3 to 4 seconds before any change in tailpipe temperature could be noted after a change of the amplifier control. Formation flying would be extremely difficult when using the afterburner as the pilot has no means of varying power short of shutting down the afterburner completely."

"Speed brake operation was excel-

lent because of the location of the switch and immediate actuation of the brakes. Retraction of the brakes was considered slow."

"Emergency systems were excellent because of the simplicity of the systems and ease of operation. Special note should be given to the emergency boost system. Although, it was not considered necessary to have an emergency boost system, it would be highly desirable and it is expected that such a system might be necessary under certain conditions. One unsatisfactory feature of the system was that an air start could not be made because of little or no engine windmill rpm. There was no way of starting the engine without external power and this deficiency was considered critical."

Recommendations: "It was recommended that:
1.) Aileron breakout forces be lightened.
2.) The elevator stick force reversals be corrected.
3.) The oxygen pressure gauge be relocated so the pilot may read the gauge when the throttle is forward.
4.) The diameter of the control stick grip be reduced.
5.) The cabin thermometer and oil temperature gauge be interchanged. This will give a better engine instrument arrangement.
6.) Pilot visibility be improved.
7.) Bullet-proof windshield distortion and reflection be eliminated.
8.) Taxi lights be improved.
9.) An indicator or warning for dive brakes be installed.
10.) A means of dimming the landing gear warning light for night flying be provided.
11.) The time lag of the afterburner amplifier control be decreased,
12.) Reduce the retraction time of the speed brakes.
13.) Operation of the emergency pump and stand by switch be reversed.
14.) Some provisions for making air starts be incorporated.

YF-93A 48-317 Explosion: The Air Force Phase II testing ended abruptly during the 44th flight of the number one YF-93A, the last scheduled flight of the Phase II program, on 5 June 1950 when 48-317 experienced an explosion in the aft fuselage. The AF accident report has not been

LANDING DISTANCES AND SPEEDS

Landing	IAS at 50 ft. Obstacle Knots (mph).	Total distance Over 50 ft. Obstacle ft.	IAS at Touchdown. Knots (mph).	V_T at Touchdown Knots (mph)	Gound Roll ft.
1	172 (198)	8,780	137 (157)	126 (143)	3,855
2	100 (104)	6,380	143 (164)	131 (151)	4,715
3	172 (198)	6,240	136 (156)	125 (144)	4,590
4	145 (167)	6,030	122 (140)	115 (132)	4,580
5	151 (124)	6,980	127 (146)	117 (125)	4,785

located as it appears that it never made it to the official archives, but it is known that Major Everest was flying the aircraft at the time and the aircraft was in a heavy weight configuration for takeoff and landing tests.

According to the NAA report, a fire warning occurred during flight while the afterburner was in operation. Major Everest ceased afterburner operation and noted that the fire warning light went out. The afterburner was ignited twice again, but no fire warning was displayed, leading Major Everest to believe that the previous fire warning was a false warning. The aircraft was landed and taxied into position for another takeoff. The afterburner was ignited during the takeoff roll when an explosion occurred resulting in severe damage to the aircraft.

The cause of the fire and explosion was determined to be a broken afterburner fuel manifold drain line. This drain line was under the same pressure as the afterburner fuel manifold when the afterburner was operating as the check valve was located at the firewall. The rupture in the drain line allowed the high pressure fuel to be sprayed on or near the hot turbine wheel housing.

The line had broken just forward of the bracket that supported the line at the turbine wheel flange. The line had been machined down slightly in order to adapt it to the fitting which connected it to a flex line. The rupture took place at the end of the machine cut. No radius was provided for the undercut portion and it was believed that local stress concentrations had occurred in that area by vibration and the weight of the flex line.

In order to prevent a similar occurrence with the number two aircraft 48-318, the afterburner drain line was disconnected and the drain connection on the manifold capped. This, however, was only a temporary provision until parts for a permanent modification were designed. The present drain line was to be removed and a flexible steel line installed from the manifold to the firewall. NAA also recommended that a high temperature resistant check valve be located at the manifold drain connection instead of at the firewall as on the original installation.

The damage to the aircraft was significant. The aft fuselage structure was damaged beyond repair, the shroud and aft fuselage section of the afterburner collapsed and the number three combustion chamber outer casing was broken. The engine and afterburner had to be sent to

Pratt & Whitney for repairs.

The damaged aircraft had to be returned to the NAA Inglewood facility at Los Angeles International Airport for major repairs and modifications.

At this time, it was decided to modify the aircraft to the conventional, side-scoop intake configuration as the flush inlet configuration resulted in unacceptable performance and the aft fuselage drag was much higher than the wind tunnel results. Overall performance was well below what had been predicted and current production aircraft could outperform it in nearly every way.

Modifications Made to 48-317: After the 5 June 1950 accident, NAA did a major rework on the forward fuselage and redesigned the aft fuselage in an attempt to improve performance. These changes were only done to the number 1 aircraft, the number two aircraft remained unchanged.

To improve inlet performance, ram type inlet ducts replaced the flush inlets. These ducts protruded outside of the mold line and the leading edge was moved forward. It is rarely noted, but the scoop inlet of the modified first YF-93A was not a "scab on" over its original flush inlet. The entire inlet geometry was changed by the modification.

Both inlets were equipped with boundary-layer bleed ducts which removed the boundary-layer air at the inlets and discharged it at exits on the fuselage aft of the inlets. In the case of the submerged inlet the exit spilled the boundary-layer air at right angles to the air flow over the fuselage, while the exit on the scoop inlet spilled the air parallel to the external air flow.

Each had different entrance areas, with each inlet and exclusive of the boundary layer bleeds, were 240 square inches for the submerged inlet and 215 square inches for the scoop inlet.

The entrance of the scoop inlet was farther forward on the fuselage than that of the submerged inlet, resulting in a diffuser length of 14.6 feet compared to 10.0 feet for the submerged-inlet diffuser. Both diffusers dumped into the identical plenum chamber. A plenum chamber is a pressurized housing containing a fluid (typically air) at positive pressure. One of its functions is to equalize pressure for more even distribution, compensating for irregular supply or demand.

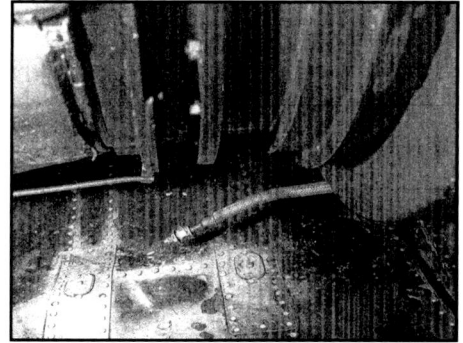

Above, broken afterburner fuel drain line which caused the 5 June 1950 explosion. (NARA) Below (top drw.), original flush inlet and bleed air ducts used on 48-317 and all the time on 48-318. (NACA) Below (bottom drw.), ram inlet and revised scoop bleed air ducts retrofitted to 48-317 after 5 June 1950. (NACA) Bottom, ram air intake on 48-317 on 15 September 1950. (Ginter collection)

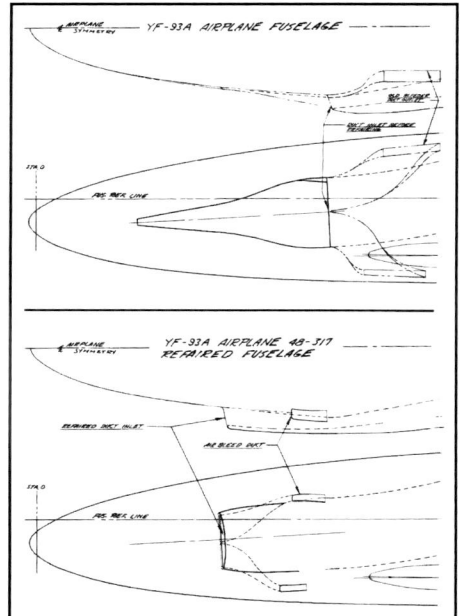

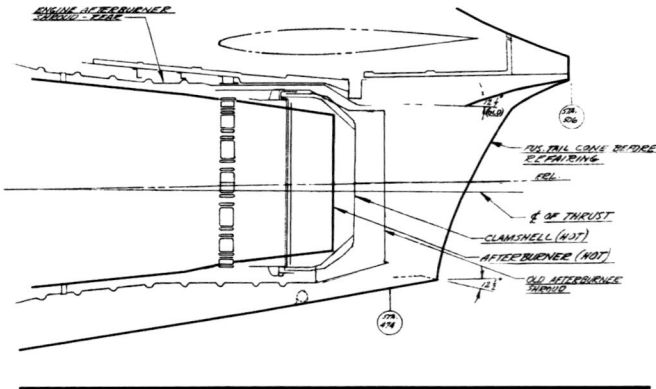

YF-93A AIRPLANE 48-317 FUSELAGE

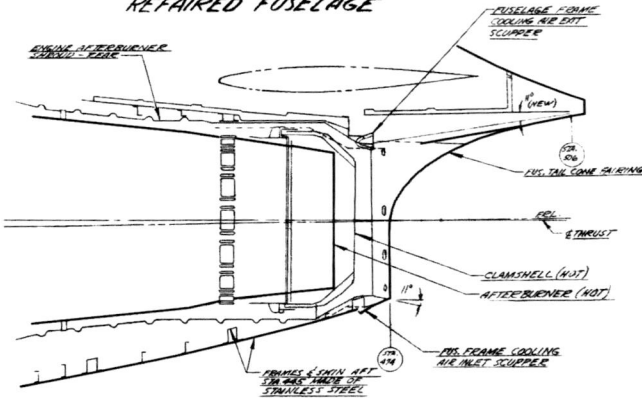

YF-93A AIRPLANE 48-317 REFAIRED FUSELAGE

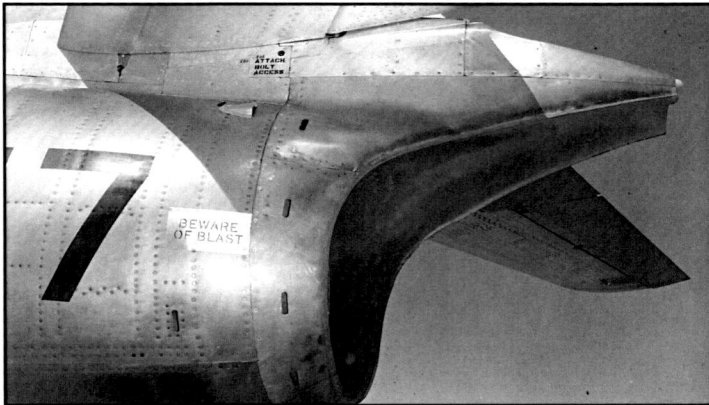

The change to the inlet duct required the relocation of equipment, which was attached to the side of the planum chamber in the direct path of air from the duct, to a position between the top of the fuel cell and the structural shelf (approximately 10 inches above the fuel cell). A closed compartment was formed by the shelf, tank and a plate to obtain a smooth flow.

In an attempt to improve performance by reducing drag and thrust lost, the aft fuselage was refaired. The aft fuselage was modified with a smaller cross sectional area at the engine exhaust nozzle by refairing the fuselage aft of station 378.5. The refairing was made over 95.5 inches of the aft fuselage. Cooling air in flight was obtained from two fixed ducts. Additional cooling on the ground was obtained by two suck-in type inlets which closed in flight. These ducts were also located on the aft fuselage.

The thrust line was above the F.R.L. (Fuselage Reference Line) with the refaired fuselage which would have resulted in a pitching moment when power was added. To solve this problem the thrust line was changed by rotating the engine about the engine main trunnions.

In addition to improve stability, a spring balanced six pound per G bob weight was installed. A bob weight is a weight added in the pitch mechanical control system in order to give the pilot appropriate stick force per G during a pitch maneuver.

To improve cooling of the aft fuselage, nine cooling air slots were cut in the aspirator and the support clips reduced in width to improve heat transfer. And, to improve the airflow to the engine, the plenum chamber was cleaned up to improve pressure recovery.

Test Results with the Ram Inlet and Refaired Aft Fuselage: NAA flight testing on the modified number one YF-93A resumed on 15 September 1950. With the new ram inlets and a refaired aft fuselage, the performance obtained in the initial phase of flight testing indicated that base pressure drag and external duct drag were the primary causes of low performance. Performance data obtained with these modifications showed a very definite perfor-

At top left, drawing of the original aft fuselage for flights through 5 June 1950. (NAA) Above left, drawing of refaired fuselage after the accident rebuild. (NAA) At left, rebuilt aft fuselage of 48-317 on 9 October 1950 (flight 53) with nine cooling air slots (4 are visible) added to the modified aspirator in September. (NAA/Boeing via Mike Lombardi) Below, drawing of 48-317's original engine cooling air flow system through 5 June 1950. (NAA)

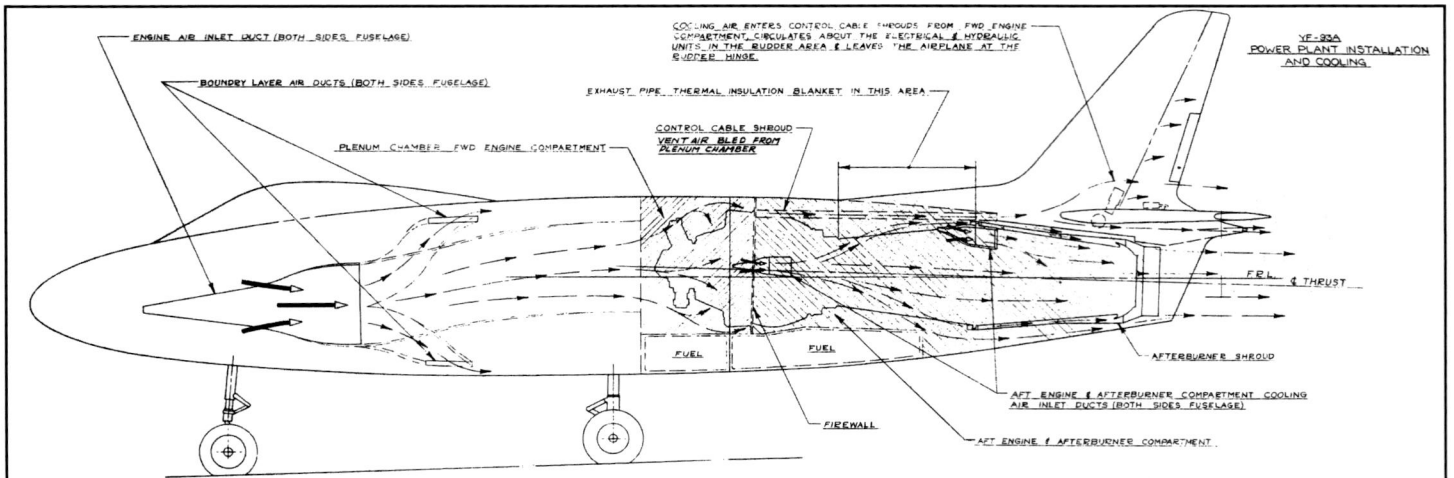

mance improvement over the original configuration (flush inlet ducts and the original ft fuselage).

In this configuration, a speed of 601 KIAS was obtained in level flight at a low altitude of 5,000 feet with augmented power, which was the highest obtained by Welch in level flight on any of the aircraft he had flown, including the F-86A and F-86D. In spite of the very high speed, the aircraft characteristics were described as extremely steady, with no apparent buffet. He also noted that the aircraft was steady even in rough air. In his opinion, the YF-93A was the most stable low level high speed gun platform that he had ever flown.

As a plus, the drag characteristics of the flush and ram type inlet ducts, and base pressure drag, could now be evaluated in flight since the aft fuselage on the aircraft were interchangeable.

The results clearly indicated that the performance evaluation of the aircraft in Phase II was premature.

Qualitative checks were made on Flight 47, 19 September 1950, at 15,000 feet, at an approximate weight of 20,900 pounds gross weight and a 20.9% CG to evaluate the characteristics of the 6 pound per G bob weight installed on the number 1 YF-93A. Elevator control forces were checked in turning flight at 330 KIAS. Accelerations up to approximately 3.5 G, where stall occurred, were applied during this test. Pull forces with stable gradient were obtained up to the stall speed. Welch considered from these tests that the elevator stick force gradient in accelerated flight was entirely satisfactory. The stick free dynamic stability was checked by applying approximately 1.5 G and releasing the stick. The resulting oscillation was damped in 1.5 cycles.

On 27 September 1950 Major Everest had an opportunity to fly the modified aircraft on its 52nd flight. It is not known what maneuvers he performed during the flight or what impression the modifications had on him since neither were documented.

Performance testing continued on 9 October 1950 on Flight 54 where an augmented power speed at 26,500 feet showed a maximum speed of 563 knots (0.941 Mach). During this flight, a non-augmented climb was made to 20,000 feet where the climb was continued to 44,000 feet with augmented thrust. The indicated rate of climb at termination was approximately 1,200 feet per minute,

although the engine was operating 900 RPM below the 11,000 RPM rating.

A seven mile level flight run was made at 3,500 feet with afterburner augmented military power at 572 knots shown on the pilot airspeed indicator. This is 611 knots TAS. As stated in the report, the trend of high speed curve for the aircraft in its present configuration indicated that at 2,300 feet an airspeed of 613 knots could be attained.

Of interest is that this data was classified Secret, with no explanation given to the reason why.

But there were also new problems. As performance increased so did the temperature of the aft fuselage around the afterburner.

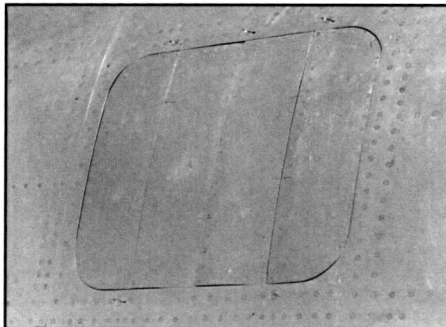

During the ram intake and tailcone modifications suck-in doors were added to the fuselage to increase the air flow to the plenum during ground operations and low speed flight. Above left, doors closed. Above, doors open. (both NAA/Boeing via Mike Lombardi)

Ground cooling tests of the refaired fuselage installation indicated satisfactory cooling could be obtained. On Flight 46, completely satisfactory cooling was realized during a climb to 34,000 feet at military power. At this altitude the afterburner was ignited and the climb continued to 42,000 feet at which point the afterburner was shut down. Data revealed that the temperature of the lower portion of the frame at Fuselage Station 469 (FS 469) rose rapidly after the afterburner ignition

HIGH SPEED PERFORMANCE COMPARISON AT 15,000 FEET

Configuration	Augmented Power (Knots)	Military Power (Knots)	Normal Rated Power (Knots)
Original Flush Inlets Original Aft Fuselage	564	483	426
Refaired Flush Inlets Original Aft Fuselage	565	504	440
Ram (Scoop) Inlets Refaired Aft Fuselage Minimum Obstructions in Plenum Chamber	576	551	481
Estimated from NA-48-845 Preliminary Performance Calculations for YF-93A, dated 30 July 1948	590	564	530

RATE OF CLIMB PERFORMANCE COMPARISON

Configuration	Augmented Power (Ft/Min)			Normal Rated Power (Ft/Min)		
To	10,000	20,000	40,000	10,000	20,000	30,000
Original Flush Inlets Original Aft Fuselage	5,100	3,400		2,200	1,250	
Ram (Scoop) Inlets Refaired Aft Fuselage Minimum Obstructions in Plenum Chamber	8,350	6,000	2,550	3,000	2,100	1,100
Estimated from NA-48-845 Preliminary Performance Calculations for YF-93A, dated 30 July 1948	9,500	7,250	2,300	4,250	3,080	1,850

Above, afterburner overheat damage after flight 47 on 21 September 1950. Below, aft fuselage fuel vent, commonly called the "Sabre Drain". The "Bump" was added to regulate pressure. (both NAA/Boeing via Mike Lombardi) Bottom, overhead view of 48-317 with new ram intakes and slats extended. (NAA/Ginter collection)

and exceeded the 600°F limit within two minutes. In level flight runs at 15,000 feet during Flights 46 and 47, with the after-burner operating for 3 minutes, the frame temperature reached about 400°F, but did not stabilize.

In an effort to provide more cooling air over the lower portion of the FS 469 frame, the configuration was modified prior to Flight 48. Climbs were made with the afterburner operating for five minutes up to 25,000 feet during Flights 48, 49 and 50, and the temperature remained below 600°F. However, in an afterburner climb from 23,000 feet to 39,000 feet, the FS 469 frame temperature reached 800° at 35,000 feet in less than 3 minutes.

Based on data collected from the ground and flight tests, it was concluded that the cooling problem of the FS 469 frame was present only during afterburner operation at high altitudes. As a result, further modifications were made to the cooling configuration in order to permit continuous afterburner operation for up to 15 minutes at all altitudes. This modification included a reduction of the shroud diameter by 0.5 inches in order to pump air over the frame, and holes added in the skin to circulate air in the hat section around the frame.

Tests were conducted during Flight 53 to verify that the modifications would correct the problem. An afterburner take-off and a military power climb was made to 20,000 feet. At this altitude, the after-burner was ignited and the climb continued. In less than one minute, the FS 469 frame temperature exceeded 900°F and the afterburner was shut down. Inspection of the fuselage revealed heating of the steel section of the fuselage as far forward as FS 450. It was believed that a reversal of exhaust gas occurred as soon as the afterburner was ignited. This hot gas flowed forward between the shroud and the aspirator fairing.

Additional modifications were needed to improve the cooling. These changes involved closing the gap between the shroud trailing edge and the tailcone inner fairing, removal of the spring clips between the fairing and the frame at FS 469, the addition of two holes in the upper section of the tailcone fairing, an increase in the size of the holes aft of FS 469 from 2.0 inch by 0.5 inch to 2.0 inch by 1.0 inch, and the addition of scuppers over all the openings in the fuselage skin in that area.

During the augmented power climb from 20,000 feet on Flight 54, the after-burner was on for 10.5 minutes (the longest period of afterburner operation thus far completed). Although some improvements were achieved in that the FS 469 frame temperature did not exceed 740°F, it was noted on inspection of the fuselage after the flight that nearly all of the structure had been overheated as far forward as FS 400. It was believed that this occurred because of the lack of cool-ing airflow through the aft fuselage due to inadequate ejector pump action.

Performance data was obtained dur-ing Flight 55 on 9 November 1950 to eval-uate the effect of shortening the refaired aspirator. Shortening the aspirator changed the diameter from 27.75 inches to 30.5 inches. Results showed good cor-relation with data obtained with the previ-ous refaired aspirator configuration.

On Flight 56, portions of the alu-minum alloy frames at FS 429 and FS 437 were cut off one inch from the skin. Steel angles were installed on these frames with a 0.75 inch overlap. It was planned to eventually replace them with an all steel frame. In addition, insulation material of asbestos and aluminum foil was installed between the frames from FS 420 to FS 445 to prevent excessive temperature of the aluminum skin. The blanket ran from the lower longeron on one side over the

top to the lower longeron on the opposite side. This was the last NAA test flight on the YF-93A program for 48-317.

It was planned that for future flights the afterburner shroud was to be reworked to provide more clearance between the shroud and the fuselage frames and thereby eliminating direct contact of the shroud with the frames from FS 420 to FS 445.

Delivery to USAF: No flight logs have been located for either of the YF-93As. It is known that ship one, 48-317, was flown 59 times for a total of 47 hours during both Phase I and II and the follow-on testing. The number of flights and hours flown on the second YF-93A, 48-318, are unknown.

YF-93A 48-317 was made available for delivery to the USAF on 14 January 1951 and was accepted and delivered on 5 February 1951 at Moffett Field, CA, and immediately transferred to NACA. YF-93A 48-318 was made available for delivery to

Above and below, head-on view of 48-317 on 26 September 1950 after the ram intakes were installed. (NAA/Ginter collection) Bottom, 48-317 over North Base, Edwards AFB, CA. Note wing tip test booms and the pitot boom below the capped-off flight test boom. (NAA/Boeing via Mike Lombardi)

Above, ship two, S/N 48-318, was used as the weapons test airframe. It is seen here at North Base, Edwards AFB, CA, on 16 June 1950 loaded with 8 5" HVAR rockets. Note 20mm gun ports not seen on 48-317. (Craig Kaston collection) Almost no photos of 48-318 while at NAA or the USAF exist. Below, 48-318 tail and aft fuselage under construction on 2 March 1950. Note original aft fuselage and exhaust aspirator which it flew with throughout its career with NAA, USAF, and NACA. (NAA/Boeing via Lombardi)

the USAF on 26 February 1951 and was accepted on 26 February 1951 and delivered on 5 June 1951 at Moffett Field, CA, and immediately transferred to NACA. The date the aircraft were transferred to NACA is from an Ames report, several other dates are listed in various other documents.

AF Weapon Testing: It is believed, based on very limited records and personal diaries, that between 30 June and 8 July 1950, pilots of the Air Proving Ground Command and various other Air Force pilots flew the three competitive aircraft, the McDonnell XF-88A, the Lockheed XF-90 and the North American YF-93A to evaluate their weapon systems.

Other than the second YF-93A 48-318 being used with the original flush inlet ducts and the original aft fuselage, no records have been located detailing the test program or the results except for a brief paragraph found in the Narrative History at the National Museum of the US Air Force. It is believed that Col. Fred Ascani and Capt. Murray were assigned to the weapon systems test program. Both received YF-93A pilot checkout during the Air Force Phase II program.

"In the evaluation, the Air Proving Ground Command pilots concluded that the YF-93A had insufficient range and endurance for the role. They felt it could not be successfully operated without the afterburner at altitudes above 25,000 feet, that the maximum altitude with afterburner operating was only 32,000 feet, and the afterburner consumed too much fuel at low altitudes."

"Furthermore, the evaluation flights revealed that airspeed deteriorated rapidly during maneuvers, even with the engine at full thrust. In their tests, the maximum limit speed was Mach 0.94. Above Mach 0.70, tracking was difficult because of snaking. Wing tip stalls and mild stick force reversals were encountered during normal pull outs from gunnery and bombing runs. They also indicated that with the landing gear and flaps down, and the speed brakes extended, the aircraft could not maintain level flight."

Unfortunately, the data is presented in a manner which makes its value questionable. For example, the maximum limiting airspeed of Mach 0.94 does not specify an altitude or a configuration. It is known that, based on the unpublished Phase II Stability and Control Tests results report, that the maximum level flight airspeed was Mach 0.939 at 20,000 feet with afterburner and Mach 0.750 at 25,000 feet with Mil Power (afterburner off). The Stability and Control Tests were flown in a clean configuration; the Weapon Tests were flown either with bombs or rockets or clean.

In addition, there is no mention of stick reversals in pull-outs, any snaking or rapid airspeed deterioration during maneuvers in the Stability and Control Tests. In the Stability and Control Tests, the only mention of stick reversals occurred in the stall. The configuration of the Weapon Tests is again unknown.

Were the Weapon Test results valid? Like the AF Phase II tests, they were flown very early in the program on a configuration that was not representative of the aircraft being proposed to the AF.

Proposed Horizontal Tail Configurations: Flight tests with the YF-93A and F-86 series aircraft with conventional tail configurations indicated overshoot tendencies during high Mach number pullups caused by the horizontal tail being in the wing wake. Data also indicated that the tail drag of the YF-93A was excessive. NAA investigation of these problems by wind tunnel tests and all-movable tail tests on F-86A 47-119 led to NAA recommendation of various tail positions and the all movable tail configuration to be flight tested on the YF-93A.

By lowering the horizontal tail 9.625 inches and moving it forward, the exit area could be reduced considerably and the fuselage overhang shortened. This modification would lower the base pressure drag, reduce the possibility of jet interference and reduce fuselage tail intersection drag through improved filleting. It was expected that the resulting performance from this modification would

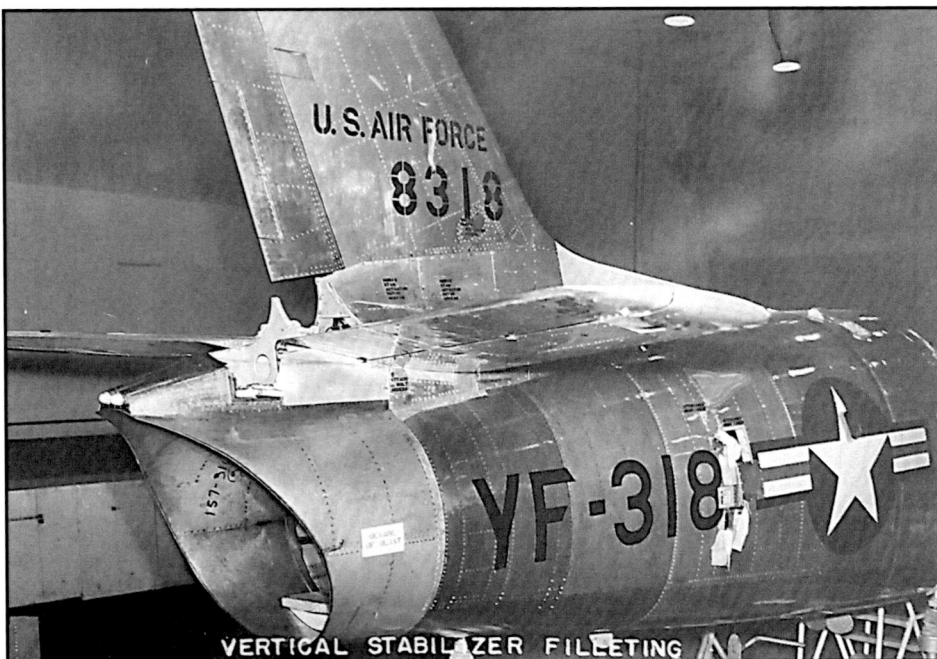

VERTICAL STABILIZER FILLETING

result in the original estimates being met and in some cases could exceed estimated values. This position had very little affect in improving the overshooting tendencies and did not change the general stability characteristics.

Lowering the horizontal tail 40.75 inches and moving it forward 28.5 inches resulted in similar drag characteristics as those obtained with the 9.625 inch lowered tail. However, the stability input from the tail would always be stabilizing, alleviating the overshoot problem.

In late October 1950, NAA proposed that the horizontal stabilizer on 48-317 be lowered ten inches and moved forward to improve maneuvering and performance. This proposal was disapproved by the AF.

Proposed All Movable Horizontal Tail:
Flight tests with an experimental all-movable horizontal tail made on F-86A 47-119 indicated improved control of the aircraft. NAA desired to modify the YF-93A to use this as it eliminated mass balances and fixed linkages to the horizontal stabilizer, which were subject to buffet and to reduced overshoot tendencies.

Again, a brief paragraph found in the Narrative History at the National Museum of the US Air Force further states that "after the weapon testing the flight test program was briefly resumed. The second YF-93A was returned to North American where the APG-30 radar, the A-1 gun sight and the ARN-6 radio were removed and an all movable horizontal stabilizer was installed. Both aircraft were to have been readied for flight again in September, but the first aircraft was not returned to Edwards for additional flights until October."

This has not been confirmed, as no reports or photos have been located indicating that the all-moveable horizontal stabilizer was ever installed.

Proposed AF Phase II Reevaluation:
The Evaluation Board's appraisal, announced on 15 August 1950, gave first place to the XF-88A, but made it clear that none of these aircraft possessed the range and endurance to perform the mission. They represented little, if any, improvement in overall combat performance over the Republic F-84E and none over the North American F-86.

The YF-93A was no longer being considered as a penetration fighter, but it appears that the Air Force was still interested in it.

YF-93A
HORIZONTAL STABILIZER
POSITION LOWERED 9⅝ IN.

On 26 September 1950, Lt. Col G. F Keeling, the Chief of Aircraft and Missile Procurement Division, requested that the Flight Test Division pilots who flew the YF-93A aircraft in the penetration fighter evaluation again fly the aircraft upon conclusion of the short flight test program then in progress by NAA. This was requested because of the changes NAA had made to the aircraft, including the new duct design and refaired tail section which had increased the performance considerably.

It was also requested that a short memorandum report be written on the pilot impressions on the differences of

handling characteristics and performance characteristics of the aircraft with the major modifications.

On 2 October 1950, Major Robert F. Fackler, Chief of the Control Section, Flight Test Division, approved it. At this point, the water becomes very muddy as with much of the YF-93A records there is conflicting information as to what happened next. One document states that the Air Force conducted 3 test flights for a total of 5 hours and 13 minutes on the modified YF-93A number one aircraft between the 18th and 25th of November 1950. The pilots' names are unknown. Another document states four flights were

YF-93A
HORIZONTAL STABILIZER
POSITION LOWERED 40¾ IN.

made by Edwards AFB pilots on 20 and 21 November 1950. It is possible one of these flights was a pilot checkout and therefore not considered a test flight. Tests included check climbs with and without afterburner operating, a speed power at 30,000 feet and speed points at 35,000 and 15,000 feet. In addition, a high speed dive was performed. Additional tests were to be performed by Wright Patterson AFB pilots. These pilots were expected to report to Edwards AFB on 27 November 1950 for the purpose of flying rechecks of the performance test points. Without a flight log and written reports, it is impossible to determine what actually happened. The flight test program officially ended in December 1950.

Development Tests at NACA Ames: With the end of the Air Force testing and lack of interest in further use of the YF-93A's, both were transferred to NACA Ames.

NACA Ames, now called the Ames Research Center (ARC), is a major NASA research center at Moffett Federal Airfield in California. Ames was founded to conduct wind-tunnel research on aerodynamics, and in the 1950s had important flight test research missions involving aerodynamics, inlets, and propulsion investigations.

According to Ames the first aircraft, 48-317, arrived on 14 February 1951 and would become NACA 139. The second YF-93A arrived 4 months later on 6 June 1951 and was assigned the call sign NACA 151. It should be noted that a number of dates associated with the delivery of the aircraft have been found in various documents and the dates supplied herein appear to be correct. A request for the NASA flight records while the aircraft were at Ames was fruitless.

Due to the problems the aircraft had experienced with its NACA flush inlets and the high drag of the propulsion system exhaust and aft fuselage, it was the ideal flying testbed to investigate why NACA wind tunnel testing had gotten it so wrong.

Inlet Tests – NACA Flush Vs Scoop: NACA Ames conducted flight tests on the two different YF-93A inlet configurations, a NACA flush (technically called a submerged divergent-wall) inlet, and a scoop inlet to determine their characteristics. Measurements were made of the pressure-recovery characteristics of the inlets and the overall airplane drag for each configuration. The investigation covered tests of the inlets in the Mach number range of about 0.50 to 0.98 and over the mass-flow-ratio range available by varying engine speeds from idle to full power.

The engine remained the same, a J48-P-1 centrifugal-compressor engine.

As stated earlier, both inlets were equipped with boundary-layer bleed ducts which removed the boundary-layer air at the inlets and discharged it at exits on the fuselage aft of the inlets. In the case of the submerged inlet, the exit spilled the boundary-layer air at right angles to the air flow over the fuselage, while the exit on the scoop inlet spilled the air parallel to the external air flow.

Each had different entrance areas exclusive of the boundary layer bleeds, of 240 square inches for the submerged inlet and 215 square inches for the scoop inlet.

The entrance of the scoop inlet was farther forward on the fuselage than that of the submerged inlet, resulting in a diffuser length of 14.6 feet compared to 10.0 feet for the submerged-inlet diffuser. Both diffusers dumped into the identical plenum chamber.

The NACA report states: "Preliminary flight tests on the YF-93 airplane equipped with a submerged inlet indicated its performance was considerably below the design estimates. During subsequent investigations, performed by the manufacturer, flight tests were made on a similar airplane which contained a different inlet configuration of the scoop type

At top left, 48-317 shortly after arrival at NACA before the large "TEST" and "NACA-139" were added to the fuselage. Note yellow tail band was added with blue NACA logo and blue outlines. (NACA) Below, left-to-right: Original NACA intake on 48-318. Flush NACA intake with boundary layer sealed (darker area) on 48-318. 48-317 ram intake. 48-317 ram intake with boundary layer sealed (darker area). (NACA)

and a fuselage with a smaller aft end. The performance of the airplane was improved by these modifications. Since the results of this investigation were not sufficient to determine to what extent the inlet change contributed to the performance increase, the subject tests were initiated."

"The submerged inlet had higher pressure recoveries throughout most of the Mach number range, but also had higher drag than the scoop inlet below 0.89 Mach number. Compared on the basis of a factor of relative effectiveness, the two inlet installations were found to be of about equal merit and the maximum level flight Mach number at 25,000 feet altitude of the airplane was about the same for each inlet."

"The boundary-layer bleeds used with these inlets were found to have considerable effect on the inlet operation. For Mach numbers below about 0.85, sealing the boundary-layer bleeds on the scoop inlet improved the low recoveries, where-

as sealing the bleeds on the submerged inlets decreased the airplane drag coefficient."

Hence, from an aircraft performance point of view, based on the differences between gross engine thrust and drag of the two aircraft, NACA concluded that there was little to choose between the two types of installations throughout the Mach number range under consideration. The results of these flight tests have almost certainly contributed to the demise of the NACA flush intake as a main source of air on fast jet aircraft.

Evaluation of Cooling-Air Ejectors: The use of afterburners with turbojet engines for thrust augmentation requires a supply of cooling air flow around the engine tail pipe. One means used to supply cooling air is the jet-actuated ejector. Since afterburners are equipped with various methods for varying their exit area, the job of designing an ejector is difficult, because when the geometry of the ejector is selected for the afterburner-on operating

Above, 48-317 with "1", "TEST" and NACA-139 added to the fuselage and all USAF markings removed. The square after "TEST" was the location of the suck-in doors. (Ginter collection) Below, aft fuselage comparison with modified 48-317 at left and original 48-318 at right. (NACA)

condition, an excessive amount of cooling air may be pumped during afterburner-off operation. This disadvantage of the jet-actuated ejector as a means of supplying cooling air appears as a loss in net thrust.

To determine the influence of the ejector characteristics on the performance of the engine-ejector combination, two cooling-air ejectors, of significantly different design, were flight tested by NACA at Ames on the YF-93 airplane using the J48-1 turbojet engine. The effect of small additional changes to the ejector were also studied. This investigation covered tests of the engine in combination with the cooling air ejector in the

flight Mach number range of about 0.70 to 0.98.

The final report concluded: "Flight tests results with the two different cooling air ejectors indicated the following:

1. Tail A [48-318], which had a diameter ratio (fuselage-exit diameter divided by tail-pipe diameter) of 1.78 and spacing ratio (distance from tail-pipe exit to fuselage exit divided by tail-pipe diameter) of 0.73, had poor net thrust performance with the afterburners off, due to excess cooling air flow. Ejector performance with the afterburner operating was better than with afterburner off.

2. Tail B [48-317], which had a diameter ratio 16 percent less than Tail A

(which reduced the cooling air flow) had good net thrust performance with the afterburner on and off. This tail did indicate an undesirable effect, however, in the fact that during the afterburner-off operation a region of reversed flow was measured in the secondary system."

This research explained, in part, the YF-93A poor performance during the Penetrator Fighter flyoff and why NAA continually modified the aspirator and aft fuselage attempting to resolve the low net thrust and high base drag the aircraft was experiencing. These findings help pave the way for the much increased performance of the NAA aspirators on the soon to follow F-100 and F-107A.

In addition to these test programs, it

Above, 48-317 prior to scrapping with rudder, suck-in doors, engine, wing tips, and slats removed. Note open access doors and deployed landing gear doors. (NACA) Below, 48-318 NACA-151 fitted with 48-317 NACA-139's tail. (Mark Aldrich collection) Bottom, left side of 48-318 NACA-151 with all USAF markings removed. (Ginter collection)

---

appears that both YF-93s may have flown chase, but the author has been unable to obtain the flight records while the aircraft were assigned to NACA, so it has been impossible to know the number of flights, hours and missions.

Both aircraft were scrapped at the end of their tender with NACA in 1953 (other sources state 1956).

NORTH AMERICAN YF-93A DIMENSIONS AND GENERAL DATA

WING		**Deflection, Maximum**	35° Up, 17°30' Down
Area	306.10 ft²	Boost	Hydraulic 27.2:1
Span	38.90 ft	Aerodynamic Balance	None
Aspect Ratio	4.943	Static Balance	Weighted Horn
Taper Ratio	0.502		Balance
Dihedral Angle	1° 00'	**VERTICAL TAIL**	
Mean Aerodynamic Chord	98.75 In	Area (Excluding Dorsal Fin)	33.46 ft²
Sweepback of 25% Chord	35° 15'	Aspect Ratio	1.714
Incident of Root Chord	+1° 00'	Taper Ratio	0.3677
Geometric Twist	2° 00'	Mean Aerodynamic Chord	55.22 In
Root Airfoil (Normal to 25% Chord)	NACA 0012-64(Mod)	Sweepback of 25% Chord	35° 00'
Tip Airfoil (Normal to 25% Chord)	NACA 0011-64(Mod)	Root Airfoil (Normal to 25% Chord)	NACA 0011(10)-64
FLAPS, Single Slotted Type		Tip Airfoil (Normal to 25% Chord)	NACA 0011(10)-64
Area, Total	32.51 ft²	**VERTICAL FIN**	
Equivalent Span, Each	79.01 In	Area	28.20 ft²
Equivalent Chord, Constant	29.63 In	Off Set	0° 00'
Deflection, Maximum	38° 00'	Dorsal Fin Area	4.31 ft²
Gap	1.00%	**RUDDER**	
AILERONS, Straight Sided Type		Area	5.26 ft²
Area, Each	16.36 ft²	Span	77.20 In
Equivalent Span, Each	108.53 In	Equivalent Chord Lower	14.11 In
Equivalent Chord, Inboard	25.72 In	Upper	5.69 In
Equivalent Chord, Outboard	17.71 In	Deflection, Maximum	27° 30' Right and Left
Maximum Deflection	15° Up 15° Down	Boost	None
Boost	Hydraulic 21. 2:1	Aerodynamic Balance	None
Aerodynamic Balance	Sealed Paddle Balance	Static Balance	Weighted Horn
Static Balance	Weighted Leading Edge		Balance
Trim Tab (Left Aileron Only)		**Trim Tab**	
Area	1.05 ft²	Area	0.58 ft²
Equivalent Span	26.98 In	Span	20.00 In
Chord, Constant	5.60 In	Chord Constant	4.17 In
Deflection, Maximum	14° Up 14° Down	Deflection, Maximum	10° Right and Left
LEADING EDGE SLATS		**FUSELAGE**	
Area (One Side Only)	17.72 ft²	Side Area	224.64 ft²
Span	155.24 In	Length (Basic)	513.00 In 42.75 ft
Chord, Constant	16.43 In	Depth, Over Canopy	82.75 In 6.90 ft
Ratio of Slat Span to Wing	0.6961	Width, Maximum	85.00 In 7.08 ft
Simi-Span (bSL / bw/2)		Fineness Ratio	6.125
Extension, Maximum	7.76 In	Deflection, Maximum	45° 00'
HORIZONTAL TAIL		**SPEED BRAKE**	
Area	46.09 ft²	Surface Area (Both)	15.29 ft²
Span	14.83 ft	**SURFACE AREA, TOTAL**	1351.96 ft²
Aspect Ratio	4.77	**FRONTAL AREA, TOTAL**	59.32 ft²
Taper Ratio	0.451	**LANDING GEAR**	
Dihedral Angle	0.00°	Main Gear, Tire Size	Dual 26x6.00
Mean Aerodynamic Chord	35.57 In	Nose Gear, Tire Size	24x5.50
Sweepback Angle at 25% Chord	35° 00'	Steering	Hydraulic
Root Airfoil (HT Station 0)	NACA 64A010	Deflection	27° 30' Right and Left
Tip Airfoil (HT Station 89.00)	NACA 64A010	Tread	135.00 In
HORIZONTAL STABILIZER		**ENGINE**	
Type	Adjustable from Cockpit	Pratt & Whitney	JT-7A J48-P-1
Area	26.28 ft²	Thrust Afterburner Off	6,250 Lbs
Deflection, Maximum	3° Up, 9° Down	Thrust Afterburner On	8,120 Lbs
ELEVATOR		Military RPM	10,950
Area, Total	12.93 ft²	**ARMAMENT**	
Span, Each	77.71 In	Guns (6)	20 mm
Equivalent Chord Inboard	16.15 In	Bombs (2)	1,000 Lbs
Equivalent Chord Outboard	7.99 In	Rockets (16)	5.0 In

ANIGRAND CRAFTWORK 1/144 and 1/72 SCALE YF-93A RESIN KITS

There are three Anigrand Resin YF-93 model kits. 1/72 scale Kit #AA-2039 contains 29 yellow resin parts, a clear canopy piece and decals. The 1/72 scale kit is also available as part of a Penetration Fighter 3-in-1 gift set number AA-3002. This set includes the XF-88, XF-90 and the YF-93. The box art for this set is reused on Anigrand's 1/144 scale Penetration fighter 3-in-1 gift set number AA-3006. The 1/144 scale YF-93A has 19 yellow resin parts and a clear canopy with decals. As a bonus, this set includes a B-36 conversion to create the Convair X-6 nuclear bomber. The YF-93A depicted in all three kits is S/N 48-317 with its original NACA flush inlets and decals. In error, the 1/72 scale kit's nose gear scissors are molded on the wrong side of the nose strut.

Below, 1/144 scale kit. Bottom, 1/72 kit with 1/144 kit in the background.